The Student's Guide to Exam Success

SECOND EDITION

Eileen Tracy

Mc Graw Hill

Open University Press

Open University Press
McGraw-Hill Education
McGraw-Hill House
Shoppenhangers Road
Maidenhead
Berkshire
England
SL6 2QL

email: enquiries@openup.co.uk
world wide web: www.openup.co.uk

and Two Penn Plaza, New York, NY 10121-2289, USA

First published 2002
Reprinted 2002
Reprinted 2004
Second edition 2006

A catalogue record of this book is available from the British Library

ISBN-10: 0 335 22048 7
ISBN-13: 978 0 335 22048 9

Library of Congress Cataloging-in-Publication Data
CIP data applied for

Typeset by RefineCatch Limited, Bungay, Suffolk
Printed and bound in Poland by OZGraf S.A.
www.polskabook.pl

The *McGraw·Hill* Companies

Contents

Preface

If you're a student in further or higher education, or preparing to become one, this book is for you. Note that I don't differentiate between further and higher levels, simply because the techniques for exam success are fundamentally the same. In fact, many of the skills in this book – from essay planning to memory tricks – are skills I also teach GCSE and A-level pupils. The difference lies not so much in the techniques themselves, but in the depth and detail with which you choose to apply them in your work.

This book will help you develop a confident and capable approach to coursework and exams in the formats most common at higher levels. That approach should also lead you to succeed in other assessment situations particular to your course.

Acknowledgements

First, a heartfelt thank you to all my students for talking to me so frankly about their experiences with exams, and to all the people who gave me their testimonials, some of which are published in this book.

I'd also like to thank James Stevenson and others who have supported my work.

The publishers and I wish to thank Frederick Fell Publishers Inc., Hollywood, Florida 33020 for permission to reproduce a section of 'The Peg System of Memory' from *Fell's Super Power Memory*, ISBN 0 88391 050 0, in Chapter 4.

I'm grateful to staff at Leicester University Educational Development & Support Centre for their generosity in sending me their student support leaflets, and to Philip Moss, Head Clerk at Oxford University, and his colleagues, for their information on degree classifications.

I'm also very grateful to Shona Mullen at Open University Press for suggesting that I write this book and for being so helpful and encouraging, and to Kirsty Reade for her enthusiasm and help with this second edition.

To Tim Waters, I'd like to say thank you for sparing time in your busy, scientific schedule to contribute the section on practical exams, without which my book wouldn't have been quite the masterpiece that it is.

My warmest thanks to Moira Munro for livening up my work with her delightful cartoons.

Last but certainly not least, I'm grateful to my husband for sustaining me through the writing process. Edward, according to my calculations, I demanded 1 laptop, 1095 hot drinks, 175kg of shopping, 730 lunches and dinners, 52 hours of discussion, 29 hours of proofreading and quite a few hugs from you to get this book under way, and you supplied all that without so much as a grumble. Well, maybe just a tiny grumble.

Introduction: Action, not anxiety

When I started writing this book, I went to a library and, as part of my research, collected ten books on how to pass exams.

As he checked the books out, the librarian glanced sternly up. I could predict what was coming, because it was May, and I look young enough to pass off as a 20-year-old. 'Now, dear girl,' he commanded me over his half-moons, 'make sure you don't waste all your time reading these books, and get down to some serious revision.'

I relate this episode because it impressed upon me how quickly people can jump to the wrong conclusions unless they seek out the underlying context first. Without this, they are likely to do more harm than good.

It also reminded me how many of us enjoy exerting power over others weaker than ourselves. Students are often singled out for such attention, since, as anyone who has ever put L-plates on their car will confirm, the learner status often arouses superior attitudes in others. People, institutions, dare I say even governments have been known to take liberties with students that they wouldn't dream of taking with other intelligent adults.

Had this chap been genuinely concerned about what he believed to be my exam neurosis, something less condescending might have passed his lips – for instance, 'What is it about exams that makes us all so anxious?' Even, 'What the hell do you want all those exam books for – you look perfectly clever to me' might have opened the channels of communication. And indeed, had I been in the alarming state he imagined, a few sympathetic words on his part might have been a life-saver. Instead, he saw my ten books, saw me, thought, 'Student with no confidence in herself at all' and proceeded to humble me further. In a kindly way, you understand.

As students, not only do most of us have to deal with other people's egos; we also have to handle our own, particularly when facing assessment. After hearing time after time what we should or shouldn't have done, and how we have failed or succeeded, it's easy to become a bit helpless. We may start to defer to others, imagining that whatever it is we are doing must be wrong, or someone else knows better. This is ironic, the aim of studying being, as they say, to develop informed opinions and become more self-assured.

Yes, well, here I am now, giving you advice in this book. Like the librarian, I too may make wrong interpretations or suggest study methods that don't work for you. Retain your critical faculties as you read: studying is essentially a personal thing. There are no rules – or very few. Plenty of students have passed exams with flying colours despite seeming chaotic in their work, simply because their attitude to exams was sound.

This is why my book is divided into three parts. Part I helps you develop ways of thinking about your work that enable you to study freely and enjoyably. Part II offers you a range of techniques that you may not wish to adopt in their entirety, but that you're invited to pick and choose at your convenience. Part III contains some very honest student testimonials to give you a deeper insight into the realities of academic life. Feel free to expand, adapt and develop your own ideas from the inspiration you gain in all these sections.

Feel free, too, to skip. This book covers a wide variety of issues related to exams: therefore, I've devised it so that you can easily dip into it in whatever way serves your individual needs. Chapters and paragraphs are summarised, mindmapped and keyworded, to help you glean their contents at a glance. This may give you some ideas for summarising in your own revision. It should also save you time reading about exam technique when you probably feel pressurised to read books about your academic subjects.

Which takes me back to the librarian. The man was quite right: reading around a subject can sometimes be a way of resisting action. Yet, as this book makes plain, the ability to stop and think marks the successful student out from the crowd. Seems contradictory? Well, there you have it: the challenge of learning is to distinguish between reflection and procrastination – and this is particularly true of education at higher levels, where you're expected to do more thinking than you ever did at school, and where it's therefore extremely useful to know when to stop thinking and start doing. As a rough guide, the time for action is

Pareto's Law

often a little earlier than you feel ready. So don't let me stop you in your tracks: you may already be more capable of starting your coursework or revision than you realise.

As you read this book, consider two things. The first is Pareto's Law, which, crudely summarised, states that the average person draws 80 per cent of their results from only 20 per cent of their effort. The remaining 80 per cent of the work they invest is largely wasted. My aim isn't to turn you into a perfect student: such a person doesn't exist. It's simply to help you develop attitudes and techniques that give you a much, much better return on your coursework and revision.

The second is my own mother's Law, which states that you shouldn't really need to revise a lot for exams if you work regularly enough through the year. Gee, thanks, mum.

Part I

States of mind for success

1

Clear your head

- The real value of higher level exams
- Helpful and unhelpful attitudes to learning
- Pressures of student life
- New ways of thinking

No great improvements in the lot of mankind are possible until a great change takes place in the fundamental constitution of their modes of thought.

John Stuart Mill

Most students fret about exams

I wonder why you're reading this book. Maybe it's because you know you could do well in your exams, and you've heard about exam techniques that might help you. Maybe that's because you're anxious about your prospects, perhaps because you've had a long absence from studying or because your past experience of exams wasn't ideal and you want to perform better this time round.

I doubt that you're feeling calm about your oncoming exams. The odds are certainly against it. Higher level exams can make students feel more insecure than they ever did at school. The stakes often seem higher: the prospect of being formally assessed, social pressures to succeed and the added pressures at college or university, make many extremely anxious in the run-up to exams.

To resolve anxiety, you have to understand what it's about. We shall start by exploding a few popular myths about failure and success. That's because you stand a better chance of reaching your goals if you can keep a clear head and a healthy perspective on your exams. One reviewer who read the first draft of this chapter remarked upon the irony that a book on exam success should start by questioning the value of good exam results, and yet a clear understanding of the real (and generally overblown) value of exam success is perhaps the single most helpful insight in enabling you to achieve it.

Society's obsession with winners

It's hard to be confident that you can get by in life without amazing grades. There is a widespread belief among student circles that those with good grades will be blessed in life and those with bad grades will suffer. This warped belief prevails despite the overwhelming evidence all around us, if we care to look, that top exam *Results don't* results don't necessarily make people happy or wealthy, and con-*define people* versely that poor exam results don't necessarily inhibit people's ability to succeed in their careers and personal lives.

I suspect the attitude has come about because grades are the only way we have of measuring young people's performance (there is a similar tendency to measure adults according to their salaries). Therefore, exam results are thought to give an indication of whether students will have successful careers.

Exam results say little about people

Results are There are two problems with using exam results as a career pre-*neither* dictor. First, they often fail to measure students' real academic *accurate...* ability. Many highly capable students underperform in exams. There are many reasons for this, though rest assured that this book shows you how to capitalise on your ability. Here are some:

- Poor study skills
- Lack of exam technique
- Fear of being tested
- Emotional problems
- Low motivation
- Poor teaching
- Illness
- Depression
- Unsuitability to traditional teaching methods (e.g. due to some learning difficulty)

Don't I need top grades to have a successful career?

No, not really – unless you intend to become an academic. Outside that sphere, you'll find that the success of your employment (or self-employment) is shaped more by your attitude than by the details of your exam classification.

By focusing purely on the exterior value of your pursuits, you may be denying yourself the fulfilment of learning for learning's sake. Or perhaps this is just the way you justify to yourself the enormous time and effort you spend on your work: maybe you're more motivated by academic matters than you would like to admit.

The failure of exam results to measure academic ability is one major reason why we have educational psychologists. If grades really measured potential, there would be no need for IQ tests, tests on verbal competence, tests on visual/spatial skills and so forth.

. . . nor comprehensive

Second, exams don't measure career aptitude. They test certain skills such as the ability to learn from classes, teachers and books and the ability to read questions accurately and to respond coherently under pressure. They also test the ability to write fast and legibly. These are all useful enough, but they are by no means the only assets that set people on successful career paths. There are hundreds. I couldn't possibly list them all, but here's a start:

- Persistence
- Resourcefulness
- Optimism
- Assertiveness
- Tact
- Social skills
- Leadership qualities
- Personality
- Enthusiasm
- Creativity
- Initiative
- Ability to follow orders
- Pragmatism
- Financial acumen
- Honesty
- Craftiness
- Reliability
- Ability to resolve disputes
- Sense of humour

- Courage
- Charm
- Contacts
- Negotiating powers

Exam results don't define careers

Good exam results certainly have their place in this list. However, it's perfectly possible to get by in life without them. In the short term, the difference between a first, second or third class degree may or may not help you get a good job. In the long term, the underlying qualities that make you who you are play by far the greater part in determining how you fare in your career. Certainly, there is no correlation between the class of degree you get and your future pay packet (just in case you were under the common illusion that exam success guarantees financial security and that exam failure spells ruin).

There are no winners and no losers

'Winners' + 'losers' = phoney concepts

Perhaps the greatest mistake that students make in thinking about exams is their tendency to connect their self-esteem to their results. They believe that exams sort out winners from losers. This makes them terrified of taking them, in case a poor result writes them off. This is sheer nonsense. Why? Simply because there are no such things as winners and losers. If you don't believe me, ask yourself whether the following people are winners or not:

- A contented housewife
- A pop star with a cocaine addiction
- A top executive who doesn't have enough time to enjoy life
- Someone who works in a charity shop

The idea that the human race can be neatly split into two clubs, winners and losers, and that grades give people direct access to the first, is so hollow that I'm surprised more people don't see through it.

Whenever you find yourself worrying about your exams, remind yourself of these two major principles:

1 Attitude matters more than grades.
2 There are no winners and no losers (just different kinds of people).

Destructive attitudes

Anyone who fails to understand this is in for a hard time. The belief that results separate winners from losers makes people neurotic in their work, or it makes them defend against failure by

Attitude matters more than grades

pretending not to care. They put on a show of indifference, to cover up their inner despair. Some make outsiders of themselves, for instance by rejecting what is offered to them, becoming withdrawn and antisocial, or even turning to crime, because they feel they can't belong to the winners' club.

The irony is that if they could forget about this bogus club, they wouldn't be so stifled by the pressure to succeed, and then they might get better results.

And what exactly does 'successful' mean?

I hear your brother Andrew is doing very well. He's just got a scholarship! He's going to be a very successful young man, don't you think?

'Success' = superficial notion

What people refer to when they talk of 'success' in this general fashion is actually something quite specific: they mean a career that brings either money or fame. You can be a kind nurse, a caring teacher, a brilliant social worker, but sadly certain people will only consider you truly 'successful' if you become a banker or a lawyer – sorry, a *top* banker or a *top* lawyer – or if you get your name in print, for instance in *Hello!* magazine.

But as the 'Curse of *Hello!*' warns us all, even those people who do impress everyone with their fine houses and fast cars often discover that their achievements make them neither happy nor healthy (as we often read the following week).

Who wants to be a millionaire?

Success = treadmill

There's an old proverb. It warns that you should be careful what you want, in case you get it. Take Andrew, the scholar mentioned above. What next? Three As at A-level, of course. Otherwise, what will people think? Well, as the saying goes, you're only as good as your last success. If Andrew is hooked on success, he needs to keep churning out top grades. This is despite the fact that he doesn't care for his subjects and would be better off doing something else.

It's not just people like Andrew who suffer. Advertisers profit enormously from everyone's terror of being a loser. Unless they learn to build their self-esteem from the inside, people will prop up their egos with the outer trappings of success, be it top grades, impressive careers, designer labels, antiques or other popular fads.

And because many people who are driven to 'succeed' have no inner sense of self-worth, they *still* feel empty when they have acquired those trappings. Marilyn Monroe, perhaps the most ambitious of women, realised this when she declared that a career, although it was a wonderful thing, didn't keep her warm at night.

Models of success

The example of Marilyn Monroe suggests how dangerous it is to entangle, as many people do, three very different concepts: exam success, career success and happiness. There is a prevalent view (which TV and advertising are largely responsible for putting about) that happiness can only come from being 'successful' (i.e. rich and famous), and that the roots of such 'success' lie in exam success. In other words, these three concepts are thought to be causally linked, like this:

If, like many, you too carry this model in your head, think again. Exam success, career success and happiness bear some relation to each other, but they aren't interdependent. For instance, money is widely credited with buying happiness: how much, exactly, do you think you need to earn to be happy? More than, say, a bus driver or a refuse collector, surely? Richard Layard, economist and author of *Happiness: Lessons from a New Science*, draws together relevant research, with the astonishing conclusion that, in First World countries, an income per head and per annum of $20,000 (that's about £12,000) contributes to a nation's happiness, and no more. Of course, you must allow for individual variations, but as a rough guideline, you can take it that you don't need to try to be Bill Gates in order to make yourself happier. So although exam success and career success may contribute to your happiness in life, they don't define it.

Happiness is . . .

Happiness arises from many other sources, for example:

- Loving relationships
- Friends
- Freedom/emancipation
- Good health
- Living in a community
- Having children (or not)
- Keeping a pet
- Hobbies

Discard the model above and replace it with the one below. This will help you keep your exams in healthy perspective:

Exam success ≠ career success ≠ happiness

You don't have to aim for the bull's eye in order to enjoy your life. If you hit it, great: enjoy it while it lasts, because it won't last. Life is too full of changes.

Success is elusive

Students can all too easily be influenced by the hype surrounding exams. Being in the process of defining who they are and what they do, and having very little life experience of their own, they tend to adopt the attitudes of those around them. Consequently, many students set themselves unrealistic targets – or allow such targets to be set for them. As a result, they often feel disappointed in themselves, *despite their successes.*

Yes, I got good grades last time, *but*:

- I should have done better.
- My mum/dad/teachers expected more.
- Compared with mum/dad/siblings/model cousins/classmates my results are poor.
- It was a fluke: I didn't deserve to do so well.
- The examiner must have made a mistake in my favour – papers can get mixed up.
- Those exams were easy; at higher levels, exams are much harder.
- I only got on this course because of positive discrimination in my favour (they needed more ethnic minorities/women/ overseas applicants/students from comprehensive schools . . .).
- I only got on this course because I was privileged and went to a good school.

Failure is taboo

If success is this hard to handle, what about failure? Well, for students who believe that their exam results determine whether they become winners or losers, every poor grade feels intolerable, as the following common reactions express:

- I've let everyone down.
- I've let myself down.
- Something must be wrong with me: I must be stupid or jinxed.
- Mum/dad/siblings/model cousins/classmates did better than me: therefore, I'm bad.
- I failed; that means I'm a failure.

In our society, failure is such a dirty word that the shame, guilt and despair it causes can be simply too overwhelming. Rarely do students realise that failure is normal, trust that they can deal with the consequences if it happens, and look upon it as a worthwhile learning experience. Consequently, universities are filled with students whose fear of failure inhibits their work. They fret so much about the outcome that they can't think. They panic. The panic makes them freeze and so they miss important deadlines, seminars, lectures and tutorials. They shun their desks and turn away from libraries – a tactic which, ultimately, makes them feel worse.

①
→ *freezing*

The same fear drives others to work too hard. They sit up all night swotting over unnecessary topics. They can't concentrate any more. They worry about this. They try to compensate by working more. Some make it. Others get ill. A few drop out. All because they believe the myth that exam results separate winners from losers.

②
→ *swotting*

It's not very surprising that some can't tolerate the pain and, tragically, commit suicide.

Pupils' obsession with grades

Freezing or swotting are responses that many students learn early in their school careers. These tendencies are exacerbated by the crude ethic of hard work spread by certain parents and teachers.

'The harder you work, the better!'

Pick up a book like this on how to study and the first message you'll read is that good results arise from working *wisely*. Quite where the idea of hard work comes from nobody knows, for it certainly isn't true. There's no doubt that learning is hard at times, but it's also good fun: it can be interesting and fulfilling. Perhaps this hard work mentality comes from our puritanical school ethic ancestry. My theory is that some adults who had a hard time in their own childhood quite enjoy getting their own back on the next generation – or simply don't know how else to present learning other than as drudgery.

Destructive
'work hard'
school ethic

Whatever the reason, here's how it works: students are told they should work hard. They feel guilty that they're not working hard enough. They think they must be bad. This either makes them try harder, and harder, and harder … or it puts them off entirely. Either way, they see work as a huge sea into which they must plunge at the risk of drowning. Some hope that by sheer determination they will make it to dry land. Others fear this swim so much that they don't even dare to dip their toe in the water.

> ### Won't I have to work harder than I did at school to get a good result?
>
> No. You will have to do some hard work, but you should also balance your work with other activities, to keep a healthy perspective on your exams.
>
> By using the techniques in this book you will work so much more efficiently anyway that you can expect to reduce your workload by about 30 per cent, and still get a better result for it. You will also find the work more enjoyable.

And then, with typical human generosity, they may pass their neurosis on to the next generation.

Learned helplessness

Throughout their schooling, children are presented with a mass of knowledge not only to absorb, but also to organise, structure and regurgitate in God knows how many different forms. Proven study strategies, like the speed-reading, mapping, memory and keywording techniques explained in this book, save time and boost grades. Sadly, few schools teach them properly, if at all.

Study skills

Strong intellects don't suffer much (though they may overwork a bit). Inarticulate teenagers, however, flail about, shun their desks, lose their books or fall ill to escape from the realisation that they don't know how to plan an essay, write a conclusion, interpret questions or sit exams. They don't know how to study, and the clock is ticking away.

What do they do? Many reach for the study notes, or get their teachers to spoon-feed them essay plans. Some have their coursework done for them, or plagiarise from their sources. The Internet is scoured for essay papers that can be copied. This behaviour is sometimes encouraged by their elders: I've seen enough essays written by parents, and I've observed enough teachers sitting at

→ *panic*

the computer working through their pupils' coursework, to be wise to the fact that adults are just as prone to panic as the children in their charge.

Pupils learn to hate learning

It's quite perverse, really: instead of trusting that children want to learn but realising they often lack the tools or stamina with which to learn effectively, many schools mistakenly assume that children

know how to learn but that they *won't want to unless they're forced.*
They are quickly proved right: the children in their care become
disheartened. Once their responsibility for their own learning
is stripped away from them, children start to lose their innate
curiosity and their natural thirst for knowledge.

Yet, as a baby, you didn't get prizes for learning to walk or talk.
You wanted to do these things for the sake of doing them, not for
the rewards adults gave you. You were interested in the activities –
you could see the point. So you tried, and failed, tried and failed,
thousands of times. Failing wasn't a traumatic experience. It didn't
make you give up. No one thought less of you for making mistakes.
You weren't scolded: you were trusted to learn in your own time.
Which you did.

When it comes to schooling, children and adolescents are rarely
trusted in the same way to produce the best outcome for themselves. It's true that learning isn't always easy, and sometimes
children recoil from it; but instead of being helped to develop
strong inner resources to face it of their own accord, children are
usually just pushed. Many teachers and parents are also under considerable pressure, pressure to turn out successful children; so some
use any tactic – force, punishments, threats, bribes and rewards – to
make schoolchildren work. This can be extremely effective in the
short term. In the long term it's a disastrous approach, because it
turns children's interest away from learning.

Pupils are cajoled, pushed or threatened to keep doing this:

more
better
best

They learn to fear making mistakes. They start to crave praise. A
child who works to please an adult misses the entire point of education, which is to promote independence of mind.

Pupils become obsessed with results

Remember what happened to you and your classmates when you
got your work back from a teacher? You turned frantically to the
back page to see your mark. You asked everyone else, or everyone
else asked you, 'What did you get?' Very few pupils even bother
to read their teacher's comment – if there is a comment – because
they're not interested in the ideas they've written about. The
only thing that matters to them is whether they've made the
grade.

Forced learning

Children
♥
learning

But carrot +
stick kills
motivation

Children +
adults crave
grades

This tedious, competitive, results-based attitude is one that many schools actively encourage. Some teachers return work by calling out the best scorers first and working their way down (or vice versa). Some even chart pupils' performance on a public scoreboard, to humiliate low scorers into working. And indeed, schools are increasingly in the business of turning out high scorers. Everyone knows that private schools need to earn a good reputation with fee-paying parents, but even state schools nowadays have league tables to live up to, or they face a reduced pupil intake, their budgets are cut and, ultimately, they can be closed down. Unless school staff are extremely vigilant in protecting their pupils from this harsh educational climate, the pressure schools are under to perform passes straight down to pupils, and education becomes all about grades.

→ disillusion-
ment

This makes it hard to tolerate failure. If, after their best effort, pupils get less than a good grade, they feel short-changed. They may feel angry; their teacher may also be angry, or scornful.

Even those who do score a top mark and get praise for it enjoy only a brief boost to their egos. Unless they value learning for the sake of learning, their delight is temporary. They'll have to try all over again next time. It's like a wild goose chase. And it's in search of this elusive wild goose that many students enter higher levels of education.

The challenge at higher levels

Education at higher levels often draws out underlying low self-esteem. This happens because the environment and structures students encounter at these levels differ in key ways from those that existed for them at school.

School doesn't
prepare you

More expectation, less support

Beyond school

The first difference in higher levels of education is the relative absence of supervision. I'm sure you've noticed that no one here seems to be interested in taking responsibility for your work (as a rule of thumb, the higher your academic level, the less likely your personal tutor is to remember your name!).

Yet expectations are higher at student level – at least, that's what many students believe, since they are often warned that they must make a greater effort now than ever before. Sometimes this is a fair warning: some college or university courses can be extremely demanding. However, in most instances, graduates comment that

More pressure?

higher level exams turned out to be less demanding than A-levels, so this added pressure exists chiefly in the pre-exam student's mind. This isn't to say that it doesn't cause genuine anguish.

In any case, whether they are real or imagined, extra demands don't often come with extra support. Although the tide is beginning to turn, colleges and universities still tend to assume that you know how to study and that you have the motivation to do it alone.

The curse of too much free time

Free time to procrastinate

Unless they are particularly interested in their subjects, most students who hit university think it's party time. It's understandable: they've finally made it. They've got through UCAS (the university clearing house system) and, finally, after years and years of forced labour, they're in! Why work?

A tutor gives them an essay to write for the following week, and they put it out of their minds until the night before. Coursework, they decide, can always be done later. Sometimes, they misjudge how late they can leave everything, and end up having to do four or five essays in a week. It's what I call the curse of too much free time: it's difficult to get going when there's no apparent urgency.

Preoccupations

New distractions + worries

To make time management even harder, student life can be full of distractions. There are social events, extracurricular activities and parties galore. Let's not paint too rosy a picture: students can also be distracted by difficulties, such as the considerable isolation and loneliness that may come from being far from home, missing school friends, sharing accommodation with relative strangers, living in a box-like room and learning to survive on basic provisions. Many also struggle with such financial pressures that they need to get jobs to repay loans. When they're not distracted by all that, they're worrying about their future: after all, they have no idea where they will be or what they will be doing in five years' time.

Mature stresses

So far I've described pressures that come with being young. You might assume that the older you get, the easier studying becomes. And indeed, mature students may have more experience, which tends to make them particularly organised, determined and proactive. As a mature student, you may find you waste less time because you're wiser and better informed, particularly if you've been in a career related to your academic subject. Life experience also clarifies what you want and what you ought to be getting. This should make you less vulnerable to bad practice, more critical of incompetence in others and more assertive in meeting your goals.

'Mature'
pressures...

On the other hand, being a mature student carries its own difficulties. It starts with finding solutions to a host of practical problems, such as how to fund the course, or how to combine a full- or part-time job with studying. With these practical difficulties come emotional stresses. For instance, if you've given up

Downsizing

a career to go back to college, you'll know how frightening and humiliating it can be to relinquish your salary. Many mature students have to downsize quite dramatically and resign themselves to the lowly lifestyle that comes with being a student. Once you've tasted financial independence and all its associated luxuries, that can feel more like regression than progression.

Often, financial dependence makes people feel grateful and resentful simultaneously. It may also increase the pressure to get good grades. If you're beholden to a family member or a grant-

Stakes ↑

giving organisation for funding your course, you may be expected to score above a certain threshold. Or you may feel pressurised to get a particularly good degree in order to jump up more rungs on a new career ladder: you may worry that with only half a lifetime left, and perhaps a family to support or pay back, there's no time to make mistakes.

Family, though it can be a wonderful source of support, can intensify the pressure. Mature students often worry about letting down their partner or their children. Students who have no

Family
work

dependents tend not to bother much with housework, shopping and cooking, and no one cares. But studying and running a family are two almost incompatible occupations, and you may feel you are constantly failing because you're trying to fulfil these two functions at the same time.

Then there's the isolation and inadequacy many mature students complain about when mixing with mostly younger students. Practically, it has implications such as the tendency to be excluded from helpful study groups, to lack peer support, find it harder to get lecture notes off fellow students and take part in

I feel old!

the general student banter that often provides so much useful information. Mature students can be rather embarrassed about their age – particularly if their reason for returning to study is to improve a modest academic track record or, even more nerve-racking, to overcome past academic failure.

Competition

Even a strong academic record can feel worthless in competitive circumstances. Students at higher levels meet other students, specialising in the subject that they excelled in at school. If you chose psychology because you were top of your class but now find yourself among other undergraduates who all got the same grade as you at A-level, you may find it hard to keep a grip on your own sense of self-worth.

Fierce competition

I'm talking from experience. I shared tutorials in English Literature with a very brilliant student whose essays rippled with academic jargon. I wasn't able to participate in discussions around his ideas since I didn't even share his vocabulary. I started to doubt my own essays, which had earned me high marks at school, but made me feel ashamed at higher level. I had met my academic superior: it was an extremely unnerving experience. Luckily, my enthusiasm for the subject stopped me giving up.

Student rivalry is like sibling rivalry

Those of us who have siblings know what it's like to fight over the same necessities – the largest piece of meat at dinner, say. The competitive atmosphere most educational establishments foster can draw out equally primal rivalries: some students feel deeply threatened by their peers' successes, and others hesitate to succeed because they imagine their own good fortune will destroy those around them. The basic attitude is a fearful one – that success is a limited commodity, that there isn't enough to go around.

Students think 'win or die'...

This is quite wrong. Success isn't like food: it doesn't come in limited quantities. On the contrary, successful students often inspire each other: we learn by imitation of each other. Being surrounded by people at least as capable as you can be stimulating.

The superior knowledge of others

A win-or-lose attitude can make the learning game seem pointless. Even if you feel able to compete with your fellow students, you can't match the expertise of your tutors and lecturers. Your ability is unlikely to outshine that of your predecessors, contemporaries and successors all put together! However much you ponder your subject, however great your enthusiasm and impressive your field of knowledge, however much you strive to be original, your exam

...but can't win

paper isn't likely to contain anything that the examiner has not seen before and will not see again.

Books

This makes it very difficult to feel good about books. As long as they have existed, these symbols of learning have aroused strong existential fears in the human race, and have been periodically burnt. There may be times when you yourself have harboured fantasies of arson! It can be unbearably humbling to read other people's pearls of wisdom. Naively, most people imagine students love reading, but the chart below shows some of the emotions that overcome them when they look at books.

Overwhelmed	Helpless	Bored	Guilty	Undermined
This book is too big. I'll never be able to read it.	This book is too small. It can't possibly contain all the information I need.	This book is dull. I don't want to read it.	I ought to want to read this book.	I don't understand this book. I can tell at a glance that it's too difficult for me.

Inadequate	Discouraged	Ignorant	Angry	Depressed
This book is too easy. Other people can read difficult books.	This book is only the first on my huge reading list. What's the point of starting a process I can never finish?	This book contains everything I need to know because I don't know anything.	Much of what's in this book I already know. It's hardly going to help me expand my understanding of the subject, is it?	I thought I had some original ideas but they're all in this book.

As for libraries . . .

Avoid these revered places of learning if you want a quiet life free of stress. The chart below shows some of the feelings commonly engendered by libraries.

Anguish	Envy	Self-loathing	Panic	Claustrophobia
This library is full of books. Books are full of information I don't know. I'm an ant in the educational universe. Help!	This library is full of people who got here earlier than me, so they're reading the best books. I've got to make do with what's left on the shelf.	This library is full of people who are much more studious than me.	This library is half empty! Where is everyone?	I'm going to be stuck here all morning.

Disgust	Fatigue	Restlessness	Angst	Persecution
This person's snoring and that person's picking his nose. I can't possibly concentrate.	I've got so much reading to . . . ZZZzzz.	It's too quiet in here. I can't concentrate.	I'm about to find out if this library has got the information I need. What if it doesn't?	There's too much information here. I'm trying to find a needle in a haystack.

Solutions

*Too many
pressures*

The extra demands of education at higher levels – the lack of regular supervision, the added pressure to do well, rivalry with equally good students, the superior knowledge of others in all its forms – take many students completely by surprise. It's understandable that students trained to become obsessed with results can feel totally insecure about oncoming exams. A tendency to swot or freeze is likely to be exacerbated under these circumstances.

*Help is at
hand . . .*

If you recognise aspects of yourself in the attitudes described so far, rest assured that this book offers you the technical support you need to pass your exams, such as time management and revision techniques. Your educational establishment may also offer support services which you can tap (see Chapter 2). And in the meantime, you can start to alleviate exam stress *right now*.

Understand yourself

①
*Awareness =
key*

You've already completed the first step towards progress. This is to bring to the surface the unconscious fears that make you stressed about assessment and learning.

Now that you know these fears, you should find it easier to control them.

Disconnect your self-esteem from your results

Here lies the paradox: if you don't make a big issue of them, you stand a better chance of success in your exams. How can this be? The answer is simple: by reminding yourself that *you are not your grades*, you develop a more rational approach to your exams.

The more you realise that you can cope whatever the result, the more level-headed you can be in your exam preparation, and the better the outcome.

②
You are not your grades

I can't stop worrying that I might fail

The aim of this book is to make you successful in your studies, so you've already made a good start.

It may also help you to think about the implications of failure: for instance, did you know that you can resit? (See Appendix 3.)

Look around you for people who have made their mark despite poor grades. Ex-Prime Minister John Major governed the country on three O levels.

By realising the pressure isn't half as bad as you imagine, you can stop fretting and clear your head so that you start working productively (and who knows, you might even start enjoying what you do).

Work for your goals – and then let them go

A helpful attitude is to focus on the *process* of exam preparation, but let go of the *result*. In other words, work to achieve your goals while accepting whatever the end product may be. Direct your thoughts away from your exam results, cease worrying whether you will get this or that qualification, and engage your mind on the process of learning. You can't determine what happens in the future, but you can hold on to what you have: the here and now – so enjoy learning for its own sake.

③
Focus on process, not outcome

Keep the chatterbox away

If you're having persistent problems with your revision, the fault may lie with your attitude towards your inner voice. Susan Jeffers, author of *Feel the Fear and Do It Anyway*, aptly names this voice the 'chatterbox'. It's common for students to be assailed by it each time they sit at their desks. They find themselves hearing these thoughts:

* Others can sail through revision but I can only get by on sheer hard work
* I don't have time for time off – there's so much to do
* I don't think I can memorise everything I need to learn for these exams
* I must keep testing myself or I'll forget everything

④
*Ignore the
nasty
chatterbox*

Those who take the chatterbox at face value feel compelled to work like swots. Once a swot, almost always a swot, because swotting begets averagely good results that reinforce the belief that harder work is needed next time. It's a vicious circle.

If your tendency is to freeze, you may be allowing your chatterbox to convince you of the following:

* I don't care about these exams
* I'm not interested in this subject
* My social life is more important to me
* I'm too lazy/immature/unmotivated to work
* I've left it all too late
* I can't do this, I'm not up to it
* Mum/dad/siblings/model cousins/fellow students are much better at this subject than me

What can you do? Stop letting your chatterbox rule your life. Tell it to go away and leave you alone. Write the thoughts down on a piece of paper and burn them, if you like.

The parent–child–adult model

⑤
*Develop the
adult in you*

Another way to deal with intrusive thoughts is that offered by transactional analysis, one of the main schools of psychotherapy. It suggests that we behave according to three types: parent, child and adult. The parent symbolises the critical side of our natures that praises and blames. Usually, it finds fault with everything we do. When we tell ourselves, 'You're useless' or 'You can't do this as well as so-and-so', we allow our parental voice to take over.

The child is that part of us that thinks and acts immaturely and short-sightedly. When we panic, have tantrums, procrastinate or sulk, we behave in response to parental injunctions – and then provoke further criticism from the parent, which usually reinforces the childish behaviour.

The way out of this sticky situation is to call in the adult, representative of the more mature side of our natures. This voice offers reasonable, problem-solving approaches. Needless to say, it's well worth listening to (and developing) at critical times such as coursework and exam preparation.

Here's how the adult could intercept a destructive inner dialogue between parent and child:

Child: I can't do this reading. It's boring and pointless.

Parent: If you don't do it you'll fail your exams.

Child: Cheers, thanks a lot. Your vote of confidence makes me feel really motivated.

Parent: Don't be so sarcastic. You know what your problem is? You're lazy, that's what you are.

Adult [*coughs discreetly*]: Hang on, stop laying into each other. Perhaps this child is scared and upset.

Child: I am upset. All you want me to do is work, work, work. I want out!

Adult: Of course you do. You're a bit scared too, because there's loads of reading to be done, and you're worried you can't do it.

Child: True.

Adult: To help you stop worrying about it, why don't you try doing just a tiny part of it, and see how it goes? You never know, it might turn out to be less difficult than you imagine.

Child: Well, I think I can do this bit.

Adult: OK. Just have a go.

Parent [*can't resist having the last word*]: Good boy.

The 'All or Nothing' model

⑥
Reassess success and failure

This is another model that illustrates success and failure as most people see them in their mind's eye: at opposite ends of a long line. I've listed a few labels we attach to either pole – you will have heard plenty more such expressions throughout your education, I'm sure. The words in brackets show you the impact made on our unconscious minds by these terms, which might explain our obsession with them. (Note the absence of words in our vocabulary to describe a less dramatic middle ground.)

```
0%  ←————————————————————→  100%
Failure                        Success
Worst                             Best
Rubbish                     Perfection
Loser                             Star
(Death)                    (Immortality)
```

There's a problem with this model. It doesn't take into account the fact that success and failure often go hand in hand. If you're not sure what I mean, let me illustrate the process at work by giving you two typical examples of student behaviour.

Jack

Jack hopes to hand in perfect work. Here is his chance to do it: he has to write an essay for the following Monday afternoon. He resolves to get started immediately. This isn't because he is interested in the topic, but because his self-esteem is low and an A would make him feel (temporarily) that he is a better person.

Now let's enter his unconscious mind, where an anything-but-best grade spells death. Jack is unaware that he has such a deep anxiety. What he realises is that he's finding it extremely hard to write this perfect essay. He fears going into the library to start his research because he believes that, to write anything truly good, he must read every book on the subject first. This daunting task gets put off: Jack socialises by day, watches all his favourite soaps on the box and then haunts the college bar at night.

After a few days' procrastination, Jack starts to feel angry and increasingly desperate. Time is running out. Saturday passes. The library is closed on Sunday, so he can't do the in-depth research he had intended. He feels his essay is ruined before he has even started. He's a loser, there's no doubt about it now in his mind. With huge effort, he manages to start writing on Sunday afternoon, cobbling together extracts from his notes, a useful entry from an online encyclopaedia, and the various parts of his seminars that he hopes are relevant.

However, he doesn't like what he's written. It's far from perfect. He berates himself for having wasted precious time. By Monday, he's so disgusted with himself that he misses his last chance to go to the library and look up the right sources for his essay. He gets a very low grade.

Jack fails because of his desperation to succeed

Jack, drowning in low self-esteem, clutches at the straw of a potential good grade to try to prove himself a winner. This backfires: in desperation he convinces himself that he only deserves to fail. His behaviour illustrates how easy it is to yield to the attraction of opposite extremes and produce poor results in the very attempt to be brilliant.

Chloe

Here's a more positive version of the same phenomenon that shows how in certain cases students who let go of the need to be best can, inadvertently, strike gold. Chloe is, like Jack, a perfectionist who fears being annihilated by failure. She's a well-organised perfectionist though, working hard for every essay, which she starts days ahead of anyone else. She researches every theme in her essay by checking what the experts say and reproduces their views in painstaking detail. This takes her hours because it requires considerable juggling. Her marks are quite good, but not brilliant. She is constantly disappointed by this. She feels a failure. Here she is, trying harder than anyone else, for only average marks.

Chloe succeeds by letting go

Halfway through term, her despair turns to rage. She decides she can't be bothered to study any more. She thinks, 'I give up. I'll never be a top student. I don't care any more.' So she stops going to the library. She scribbles her essay at the eleventh hour. It's a botched job, based on her instincts, off the top of her head. Her essay is highly commended. 'At last,' writes her tutor, 'you have developed confidence in your own ideas.'

→ failure + success go hand in hand

Jack and Chloe show us that success and failure are not poles apart. On the contrary, they work very closely together. You may recognise this dangerous list of goals that students dream up to raise their performance, and which invariably lowers it:

- I'm going to work *all day* today/tomorrow
- I'm going to work *all week* next week
- I'm going to write the *perfect* essay

∴ unreasonable ambitions backfire

- I'm going to draw up the *foolproof* revision plan
- I'm not going to waste *any* time from now on
- I'm going to read *everything* on my list
- I'm going to go to *every* single lecture
- My tutors are going to *notice* me
- I'm going to be the *best*

These statements are uncompromising and too demanding. The highest effort is expected: nothing less will do. This is so unrealistic that it almost invariably makes students feel very disappointed in themselves. They may get an initial high if they manage to stick to these goals in the short term, but over a long stretch of exam revision, these pie-in-the-sky aspirations bring only misery. Therefore, a more realistic model of success and failure looks like this:

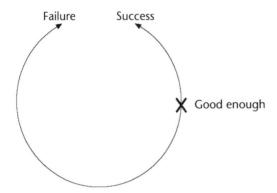

Looks a bit like a magnet, doesn't it! After all, opposites attract – it's a small step from success to failure, and from failure to success. As this diagram illustrates, it's quite dangerous to aim to be perfect. You might overshoot!

Good enough is good enough

Aim to be good enough

To avoid overshooting, try setting your sights lower, for instance aiming to be good enough. This is quite an empowering goal, since it leaves you margin for error – and as you're a student, not an expert, you need that margin. By aiming to be a *good enough* student rather than a *perfect* student, you'll find it much, much easier to cope with your setbacks. The good enough approach gives you permission to:

You'll accomplish more

- Present an outline of a thesis to your supervisor having *not* researched your proposed subject in great depth
- Start writing essays despite having *not* read every single book on the subject
- Plan a revision schedule with plenty of free time
- Be too tired to work at times
- Become ill
- Fall behind in your revision schedule and reassess
- Limit the time you spend doing things that make you uncomfortable (e.g. stay away from libraries if you work better from home)
- Try a past paper for which you feel unprepared
- Prepare for an exam without trying to learn everything about your subject

In a nutshell

I'm not suggesting you stop working or drop your ambitions: if they're realistic, keep them. However, you may not be able to reach all your goals, particularly now that you're at higher levels of education. There's so much to know that you can't win by trying to be a perfect student.

By letting go of the craving to be a winner, you can free yourself from the terror of being a loser. That makes it easier to sit exams: you can set yourself achievable targets and focus on enjoying your work. Your greater flexibility will enable you to cope well with the inevitable setbacks and disappointments of student life. It will also help you to enjoy your successes without worrying that you must surpass yourself next time.

Remember that in the long run, your attitude shapes your experiences. Make it a forgiving one.

You can be fallible without being a failure.

I'll say some of that again.

You can be fallible.

Got it?

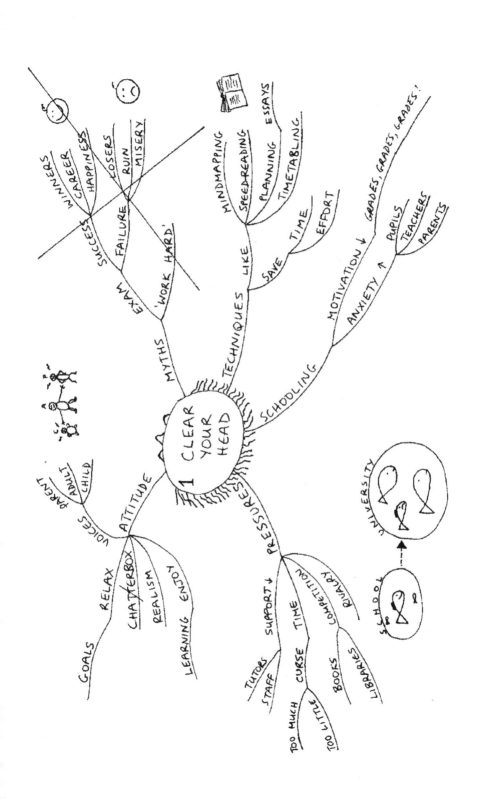

1 CLEAR YOUR HEAD

MYTHS
- EXAM
  - SUCCESS
    - WINNERS
    - CAREER
    - HAPPINESS
  - FAILURE
    - LOSERS
    - RUIN
    - MISERY
- 'WORK HARD'

TECHNIQUES
- LIKE
  - MINDMAPPING
  - SPEED-READING
  - PLANNING
  - ESSAYS
  - TIMETABLING
- SAVE
  - TIME
  - EFFORT

SCHOOLING
- MOTIVATION ↓
- ANXIETY ↑
  - GRADES, GRADES, GRADES!
  - PUPILS
  - TEACHERS
  - PARENTS

ATTITUDE
- VOICES
  - PARENT
  - ADULT
  - CHILD
- CHATTERBOX
- GOALS
- RELAX
- REALISM
- LEARNING
- ENJOY

PRESSURES
- SUPPORT ↓
  - TUTORS
  - STAFF
  - TIME
    - TOO MUCH
    - TOO LITTLE
- CURSE
- COMPETITION
- RIVALRY
  - BOOKS
  - LIBRARIES

UNIVERSITY

SCHOOL

2

Healthy body, healthy mind

- Different types of stress
- Harmful effects of quick fixes
- Physical health
- Mental health

You don't get what you want: you get what you are.

Anon

The previous chapter exploded a few myths about studying and offered you new ways of thinking about being a student, to help you keep your studies in healthy perspective. In addition, you may find it helpful to reflect on ways in which you cope with stress when it inevitably arises.

Students are often stressed...

Curiously enough, you may be unaware of being stressed, even if you are under considerable strain. Stress is like second nature to many students. Ironically, although colleges and universities are meant to be places where people learn to think, students rarely think deeply about themselves. The student rave, the college bar, the TV room or the computer can provide instant, mindless relief:

...but unaware of it

for many, that's the first and last resort, but such escapism doesn't do much for their grades.

You stand a much better chance of exam success if you can recognise stressful patterns of behaviour, realise the dangers of quick fixes and find healthy ways of dealing with stress. Therefore, the aim of this chapter is to help you promote your general well-being as part of your exam preparation.

Recognise stress when it hits you

Be aware of bad stress

I wouldn't wish to burden you with a false expectation that you should have perfect health throughout your studies. Expect to have occasional bad days and allow yourself the odd crisis, a normal and relatively harmless part of student life. However, since prolonged stress damages your mind and your health, it's important to realise when it goes beyond reasonable limits.

To help you do this, the next section explains how stress limits your physical and mental capacity. I include a few physiological explanations of stress, which you're welcome to skip.

Physical effects of stress

Stress arises when a real or perceived threat triggers a physical alarm response in us. The endocrine system, which governs the stress response, stimulates our adrenal, pituitary and hypothalamus glands to release hormones (adrenaline, noradrenaline, cortisol, testosterone and thyroxin) into the bloodstream. These stimulate us into action, mobilising our strength, speed and stamina in the following ways – many of which you're bound to recognise from your own experience of being stressed:

- Blood flow is instantly directed away from the skin, digestive tract, kidneys, liver and immune system, towards the brain, heart and muscles.
- The heart beats faster, pumping more blood to muscles.
- Blood pressure rises.
- Muscles tense up, ready for action.
- Breathing becomes fast and shallow, to increase oxygen intake.
- Pupils dilate, taking in more light.
- The liver releases stored sugar – levels of sugar, fat and cholesterol rise in the bloodstream, providing extra energy.
- Levels of platelets and blood clotting agents increase in the blood, to protect from excess bleeding in case of injury.
- Perspiration increases.

Bad stress brings you down

As you can imagine from this list, prolonged stress takes a considerable toll on the body. It's clear from the three key stages outlined in Table 2.1 that, while we may be perfectly capable of recovering quickly from short-term stress, medium- and long-term stress can be counterproductive, even dangerous.

How do I measure my own stress levels?

The more something changes your life, the more stressful it's likely to be. Some student stressors are listed below (on a life change scale of 0–100):

- Death of close relation (63) or friend (37)
- Illness/injury to self (53) or family (44)
- Cohabitation (50)
- Splitting up (65)
- Getting back together (45)
- Pregnancy (44)
- Sexual problems (39)
- Large loan (31)
- Outstanding personal achievement (28)
- End of school (26)
- Change in living conditions (25)
- Change in personal habits (e.g. more/less exercise) (24)
- Change in working hours/conditions (20)
- Moving house (20)
- Change of educational establishment (20)
- Change in recreation (19)
- Change in social activities (18)
- Change in sleeping habits (16)
- Holidays (13)
- Christmas (12)
- Minor violations of law (11)

Stress scores between 100–199 indicate a mild life crisis; between 200–299: moderate life crisis; 300 upwards: major life crisis. That's without exams.

Adapted from Holmes, R.H. and Rahe, R.H. (1967) *Journal of Psychosomatic Research, 11.*

Other effects of stress

So much for the physical effects of stress. Here's how it manifests itself in students' work:

- Performance below par
- Muddleheadedness
- Exhaustion
- Depression
- Aggression

Students' stress symptoms . . .

- Agitation
- Disorganisation
- Procrastination
- Forgetfulness
- Being persistently late
- Making up excuses
- Missing lectures, tutorials and deadlines
- Socialising too much

Misinterpretations of stress

. . . are easily mistaken for laziness

As stress signals go, many of these are fairly discreet. Many can be mistaken for laziness. Consequently, students who fail to meet targets are commonly told, somewhat unimaginatively, to 'get their act together' or 'pull their finger out'. They may even be the first to chastise themselves. Unfortunately, self-condemnation tends to make us less likely to tackle a problem constructively.

Why students don't seek help

To do so, most students need to talk to someone and get help. Yet, very few students admit they have a problem. Most suffer in silence. There's a very good reason for this. As children, many students were routinely praised for being right, and blamed for being wrong. Success was rewarded with a pat on the back; failure, with a sharp rebuff. When this happens to children, they very quickly put two and two together and equate making mistakes with being bad. In order to gain love and acceptance from their family, teachers and peers, they learn to hide their weaknesses. They may even lie and cheat in order not to get found out. Although it's an enormous effort for them, they usually manage to hand in their work and keep up with their course, albeit in a chaotic fashion.

Then, there are students who cover up their problems so well that everyone thinks they're terrific. The admiration they receive from others prevents them from fulfilling their true potential: the more they are praised, the more trapped they become. Once people learn to present a polished mask to the world, it becomes very difficult for them to seek help. The mask may come to feel like an integral component of their identity; they may lose any awareness that they are stressed. Apart from spending too much time alone in libraries or at the computer, tell-tale signs are usually psychosomatic:

- Asthma
- Skin complaints
- Recurring bouts of ill health

Physical outlets for distress

- Frequent accidents
- Hyperactivity or exhaustion
- Vomiting
- Stomach problems
- Bowel problems
- Muscular pains such as back pain
- Eating disorders
- Oversleeping (an escape from the difficulty of being awake)
- Insomnia
- Panic attacks

Table 2.1 *Effects of stress*

Term of endurance	Stress stage	Stress response
Short	Alarm	The body prepares for fight or flight, as described earlier.
Medium	Adaptation	Hormones continue to be released, blood pressure continues to rise and blood sugar levels increase – a state of arousal that the body can't maintain for very long. Unless we take regular rest at such times, we feel tired and irritable and our cognitive skills are weakened. We lose concentration and memory and lose our ability to make good decisions. We panic.
Long	Exhaustion	Raised hormone levels weaken the thymus gland, inhibiting its ability to produce white blood cells to guard against disease. Adrenal glands suffer, blood sugar levels drop and, ultimately, we collapse.

Quick fixes

Quick fixes: part of student culture

At this point, students often seek quick fixes to relieve their pain. These are widely available, and there is a certain social pressure to use them, particularly in student settings where it's part of the culture to show you're having a good time. This section shows common substances that students take to alleviate stress, and outlines the risks involved in abusing these on a regular basis.

Alcohol

Alcohol is usually regarded as a food, but is as potent as any drug since its properties make it particularly easy for the body to absorb: it penetrates blood cells within ten minutes of being drunk. The fact that alcohol is so effective in invading all fluids and tissues explains why people actually start to smell of drink once they have had a few pints, and why a breathalyser, measuring the concentration of alcohol in the lungs, indicates the level of alcohol thereby present in the bloodstream – no blood test necessary.

The powerful effect of alcohol...

Alcohol lingers in our bodies, as it can only be broken down by one enzyme, alcohol dehydrogenase. The liver contains it in small quantities, to break down the comparatively minute amounts of alcohol that arise naturally from metabolising carbohydrates in our food. Even working at full speed the liver can only clear about 7 grams of alcohol per hour. On this basis, the effects of a pint of beer take two hours to wear off.

Short-term effects are as follows:

- Disruption of central nervous system: alcohol dumbs down the brain functions that govern our social inhibitions, memory, thinking capacity and muscular coordination.
- Disruption of hormone levels, triggering excess urination and consequent dehydration.

... disrupts memory + thinking

- Excess acid in the gut.
- Disruption of the acid–alkaline balance in the body, producing lethargy.
- Dilation of blood vessels, giving a flushed appearance and producing pounding headaches.
- Increased toxicity: unless organically produced, most wines contain high levels of sulphur to ferment grapes.
- Decreased ability to eliminate toxins: for instance, lactic acid accumulates in the blood, since the overworked liver can't process it while dealing with the alcohol overload.

As well as being symptomatic of mild drug withdrawal, a hangover arises from all these effects. In the long term, alcohol can cause weight gain, muscle, heart, brain and liver damage.

Alcohol provokes anger + depression

Chinese medicine points out that alcohol has heat-producing effects: excess heat rouses the passions. Ironically, many students take alcohol to keep calm. They find it relaxes them and helps them forget their difficulties. However, they rarely realise that by drinking their problems away, they intensify their anger and depression. They also increase the risk of serious accidents when drunk.

Nicotine

Smoking 'comforts'...

Smokers' perception that smoking relaxes them or helps their concentration is quite misguided. The main reason why a smoker feels relaxed when he or she lights up is that cigarettes provide oral stimulation, in the way a comforter calms a baby. Having something to suck on provides a certain maternal reassurance. It's no coincidence that adolescents, in conflict with their parents, tend to smoke intensively. So do many students, away from home for the first time.

Apart from that, smokers smoke to relieve the discomfort of nicotine addiction (nicotine is as addictive as heroin), and because they are influenced by peer pressure and by the tobacco industry's sophisticated marketing campaigns.

While smoking gives smokers an illusion of well-being, its effects place tremendous stress on the body and mind. The following sequence of events is triggered:

1   Nicotine, being a poison, triggers the release of adrenaline into the bloodstream.
2   The consequent stress response (look back at Table 2.1) includes abnormally high blood sugar levels and raised pulse: a smoker's heart beats on average 10,000 times more per day than that of a non-smoker.
3   Exhaustion sets in, as the effects of nicotine wear off and artificially heightened blood sugar levels suddenly drop.
4   This leads to craving for further stimulation – another cigarette, a cup of coffee or a cola drink. These further inhibit the body's capacity to restore its inner equilibrium.

. . . but really adds discomfort . . .

Other effects are as follows:

. . . and impairs memory . . .

- Weakened cognitive processes: carbon monoxide, one of the gases inhaled by smokers, starves the brain of the oxygen it needs to function properly. Memory tests show that non-smokers out-perform smokers.
- Toxin build-up: smoking introduces 300 chemicals, of which 40 are poisons, into the body. Eight drops of nicotine are enough to kill a horse. Other well-known poisons in cigarettes are tar, arsenic, hydrogen cyanide (used in poison gas), acetone (a constituent of nail polish remover), benzene (produced in burning petrol), formaldehyde (used to pickle dead animals), ammonia (a bleaching agent added by manufacturers to increase the addictiveness of nicotine), carbon monoxide, cadmium and lead.
- From premature ageing, hair loss, gum disease and impotence, to the main three killers – cancer, lethal bronchitis and coronary heart disease – the long-term effects of smoking are well documented.

. . . euch!

Sleeping pills and tranquillisers

Many students suffer from insomnia, because they spend inordinate amounts of time thinking about ideas, and worrying about deadlines. Sleeping pills offer what many students crave most: an easy way to switch off the mind and sleep. These drugs are easily obtained, since they are perceived as being mild sedatives. When I was an undergraduate, my college nurse handed them out like sweets.

Sleeping pills ≠ sweets

Unfortunately, sleeping pills and tranquillisers are among the most addictive drugs on the market – used for more than a week, they start to become a difficult habit to kick. Most belong to the family of benzodiazepines (the same family as Valium). These all behave in similar ways, by disrupting the natural chemical activity in the brain with an artificial chemical override which inhibits normal communication between nerve cells. The brain's central nervous system, usually capable of producing its own tranquillisers (though not in such extraordinary quantities) is overwhelmed by these drugs, and its production temporarily ceases.

Despite being remarkably powerful, this chemical takeover doesn't provide as good an intervention as the body can produce on its own: neuroscientists can't discover, let alone reproduce, the complex chemical combinations that trigger restful sleep. Therefore, sleeping pills induce a state of sluggishness and exhaustion that makes it difficult to go to sleep the next night, producing the exact problems that they are taken to relieve. Common side-effects that can occur within two weeks are:

How the tranquilliser trap works

- Disturbed sleep
- Insomnia
- Exhaustion
- Concentration problems
- Listlessness
- Tension, fears and panic attacks
- Trembling
- Aches and pains
- Sweating
- Sickness and diarrhoea

To take these drugs for more than a few days is to risk falling into the 'tranquilliser trap' as the body and mind become increasingly restless, and decreasingly capable of calming down naturally.

Imidazopyredines, a modern development in sleeping pill technology, may be more effective and less addictive than their

→ avoid
tranquillisers

benzodiazepine counterparts as their effect on the brain's control centre is less 'scattergun'. However, even if these drugs turn out to have fewer side-effects, it's still easy to become psychologically dependent on any sleeping pill: in their early stages, these drugs appear to work so well that people who take them to get to sleep risk losing confidence that they can do without them.

If I didn't take a sleeping pill I wouldn't sleep

That could be an illusion. Curiously, half of insomniacs sleep quite well but without realising it. Under observation, they wake up insisting they haven't slept a wink. At Chicago University's sleep laboratory, volunteer insomniacs were given a placebo one night and a sleeping pill the next. They slept in both cases, but the morning after taking the placebo insisted that they had been awake all night; whereas the morning after taking the sleeping pill, they were aware that they had slept.

Conclusion: a sleeping pill won't necessarily make you sleep more than if you didn't take it, but it will make you *perceive* you slept. Therein lies its addictive potential.

Recreational drugs

The main reason why people take recreational drugs is that they temporarily boost their confidence. Unfortunately, there's a price to pay, as the 'high' they produce is always followed by a 'low', a physical and mental exhaustion that makes the sufferer crave more of the drug to feel better again. Very simply, the 'high' burns up energy, following which the body is depleted. The more stimulating the drug, the greater the 'high', and the stronger the crash that follows it. As with all the quick fixes outlined above, recreational drugs are, at the very least, psychologically addictive.

Drugs: what
goes up must
come down

From marijuana to heroin, there are so many different recreational drugs available to students, and so many widely available sources of information on the subject, that I shall focus on the most popular: namely, cannabis and Ecstasy.

Cannabis is taken for its relaxing properties which blot out anxiety: it has few short-term effects other than to dull the mind. The favourable publicity this drug receives tends to eclipse awareness of its harmful aspects. Long-term cannabis smokers suffer the following effects:

*Cannabis: wolf
in sheep's
clothing?*

- Lethargy.
- Difficulty in engaging the mind.
- Anxiety, partly due to calcium depletion (calcium is a mineral vital to maintaining a healthy nervous system).
- Paranoia.
- Irreversible changes in the brain after three years – changes greater even than those produced by three years' alcohol abuse (according to research cited by Professor Hardin Jones in his book, *Sensual Drugs*).
- Lung damage from cannabis resin and tobacco.

*Ecstasy causes
instant brain
damage*

The amphetamine derivative Ecstasy (MDMA) still receives much favourable publicity as a backlash continues against media hype of Ecstasy deaths. This is unfortunate. The greatest threat posed by this drug isn't to do with its fatality rate: it lies in the drug's instant and irreversible effects on the brain, as numerous studies now confirm. For instance, US researchers at the Johns Hopkins University found in 1999 that a monthly 400 milligrams (four tablets) of Ecstasy causes impaired verbal and visual recall, and that memory impairment increases with the amount taken and lasts at least two weeks after stopping use. Serotonin-processing neurons are permanently damaged, which inhibits the brain's integration of information and emotion.

Psychologist Oliver James offers a comprehensive overview of studies measuring brain damage by Ecstasy in his book *Britain on the Couch*. Here, in summary, are some short-term effects that you won't find listed on most Ecstasy websites (perhaps because many are compiled by Ecstasy users):

*'E' also retards
thinking +
provokes anger/
depression*

- Damage to higher mental functions: complex tasks can't be carried out swiftly.
- Irreversible damage to serotonin axons and receptors (serotonin is a feel-good chemical).
- Depression: people who take Ecstasy on a Saturday night are measurably more depressed by midweek; some become clinically depressed.
- Anger.
- Impulsive behaviour.

Long-term effects are not yet known: predictions are that, at best, Ecstasy permanently inhibits the ability to handle stress; at worst, the brain damage it causes may trigger Parkinson's disease. A 2002 study of young Ecstasy users at the University of Adelaide in Australia used brain scans and psychological assessments to predict that the drug is likely to cause permanent brain damage in middle age, with symptoms such as memory loss and psychological problems, even after Ecstasy use has stopped. Certainly, regular use of stimulants – which includes amphetamines, Ecstasy, crack and cocaine – strains the immune system, heart, liver and kidneys, and inhibits normal functions such as appetite and sleep.

Prescription drugs

Anti-depressants, stimulants, anti-psychotics, anti-hypertensives and other prescription drugs deplete the body in similar ways as recreational drugs. Many stimulants are, in fact, recreational drugs repackaged for new markets.

The truth about prescription drugs

Prescription drugs have no healing powers. Once the drug is discontinued, the problem usually returns – if it doesn't, it's usually because it would have cleared up anyway. Yet it's commonly thought that prescription drugs rectify chemical imbalances in the brain. Even if this was scientifically proven – and so far, the evidence is quite to the contrary: many drugs overpower the brain in such a way as to create new imbalances – it's an extraordinary leap to perceive drugs as the answer to psychological problems. Many problems that pills only temporarily relieve can be resolved by making suitable life changes, for example through psychotherapy. Brain chemistry is, after all, as likely to be the *correlate* of a psychological problem solution as it is to be its *cause*.

Drugs aren't the solution . . .

Indeed, in an article entitled 'A critique of the scientific status of biological psychiatry' Professor Alvin Pam points out: 'The efficacy of a drug does not prove that a particular mental disturbance is biochemically determined. For example, aspirin relieves headaches but no one contends that headache is brought about by "aspirin deficiency".'

. . . but are hyped

Despite all this, prescription drugs are greatly hyped as the answer to our problems by the powerful corporations that produce them. Drug companies spend vast amounts of money creating a 'pill for every ill' culture, spending, in the USA alone, an average $10,000 per year *per physician* in promoting their products. Though prescription drugs can be very helpful in some short-term situations, most student stresses can be relieved without medical intervention.

Hidden dangers

Medical intervention itself often comes with significant side-effects and addictive aspects. Even the new-style Selective Serotonin Reuptake Inhibitors (SSRIs) – anti-depressants like Prozac, for instance – once heralded as being almost free of side-effects, are now under serious criticism for reducing sex drive and provoking suicidal and psychotic tendencies.

Junk food

Students rarely eat a good diet. Educational establishments are famous for producing truly lamentable food, and even health-conscious vegetarian students often end up eating very un-balanced, unsatisfying meals. Mature students may have the facilities and the experience to cook good food, but they often lack the time and energy to organise healthy eating. And healthy eating certainly involves a fair amount of planning, shopping and cooking, not to mention washing up.

Students who have recently left home start making choices about their diet for the first time in their lives. Unfortunately, they tend to underestimate the relationship between good food and good health. Takeaways and ready meals are an integral part of student culture, as are crisps, chips, cakes, biscuits, chocolate, ice cream, burgers, sandwiches, sausages, kebabs and other processed foods. Their popularity lies in their convenience and often their high salt and sugar content, which gives the body an instant boost, followed by a low ebb. Like all other substances that create an artificial rush of energy, these foods are addictive, since they offer an instant physical and mental high, followed by a low that provokes more craving.

Medium- and long-term effects of a diet high in junk foods are as follows:

- Weakened immunity from allergies and infections: junk food is high in toxins and antibiotics, containing herbicides, pesticides and artificial additives that give it colour, flavour and shelf life.
- Increased susceptibility to serious conditions such as ME (Myalgic Encephalomyelitis, otherwise known as Chronic Fatigue Syndrome), due to overabsorption of antibiotics contained in junk food, or antibiotics taken on prescription to fight recurrent illness.

- Poor concentration and recall: the widespread flavouring monosodium glutamate (MSG) and the artificial sweetener aspartame, for instance, disrupt memory by inhibiting neuro-transmitter function in the brain.
- Hyperactivity: additives such as Amaranth (E123) and Sunset Yellow (E110) strip the body of zinc and magnesium, causing restlessness and anxiety.
- Malnutrition: raw ingredients have little by way of vitamins and minerals since they are grown in denatured soils, are picked before ripening, and sit in supermarket fridges and on shelves for weeks before being defrosted and microwaved (supermarkets can store apples for up to a year).

• Diabetes and heart disease, after years of excess fat and sugar consumption.

Caffeine

We're overdoing caffeine

Coffee, tea, cocoa and soft drinks are great favourites among students. They all contain caffeine, producing an artificial degree of stimulation to which the mind and body can become very addicted.

The influence of North American culture is fast making coffee a replacement for tea as our national drink. Our modern pursuit of rapid-fire lifestyles makes us increasingly reliant on caffeine as a pick-me-up. Just one cup of coffee can contain anything up to 115 milligrams of caffeine: its stimulant properties offset the exhaustion produced by late nights, stress and a diet rich in saturated fats. In fact, students can become so reliant on caffeine as a prop that they take it in tablet form to keep them going on all-night essays. Inevitably, this wears them out the next day. And many studies suggest that, while in small doses caffeine may give your memory a bit of a short-term boost, more than a cup or two of coffee a day does more harm than good. For instance, a 1981 study of college students, by US researchers Gilliland and Andress, found that moderate and high coffee consumers suffered significantly higher anxiety and depression levels than low consumers and abstainers. High coffee consumers showed relatively high levels of psychophsyiological disorders and relatively low academic performance.

How can soft drinks possibly affect my concentration?

Fizzy drinks and colas average 60 mg of caffeine and ten tea-spoons of sugar per can. These (and other sweeteners) are linked to hyperactivity. Tartrazine (E102) in fizzy orange inhibits the absorbtion of zinc, causing irritability and mood swings.

Soft drinks also contain caramel colouring (E150) which disrupts attention by disturbing neurotransmitter function, and phosphoric acid (E338) which strips the body of hydrochloric acid, essential in absorbing nutrients. Magnesium deficiency causes learning disabilities and restlessness; calcium deficiency produces anxiety and neurosis.

Coffee that isn't organically produced contains a number of toxins, as herbicides and pesticides control the cultivation of the

Coffee is toxic

coffee bean. Instant coffee is produced using various chemicals; even the decaffeinated variety contains traces of petroleum-based decaffeinating solvents. Grinding coffee releases oils that easily turn rancid. Unsurprisingly therefore, long-term use of coffee has the following effects:

- Raised cholesterol levels, from as little as two daily cups of coffee
- Damage to the lining of the small intestine
- Inhibited intake of nutrients, particularly calcium – a vital element in promoting calm
- A suspected link to cancer and other serious diseases

Tea isn't great either

Tea and cocoa are thought to be relatively harmless, and even have various beneficial properties; yet these drinks also contain caffeine: a cup of tea, for instance, contains 60 milligrams of caffeine. What's more, the tannin in tea inhibits the absorption of iron: taken regularly after meals, tea can contribute to anaemia (particularly in vegetarian women); this doesn't help the student who needs stamina around exam time.

Like junk food, a regular diet of these drinks depletes nutritional resources and compounds exhaustion and anxiety.

The Five Pillars of Health

If you abuse any of the quick fixes listed above, it would be unrealistic of me to expect you suddenly to reform. These habits are normally triggered by underlying problems; therefore I include addresses at the back of the book of organisations that can help you on a deeper level than I can here.

There is some good news: in following pursuits that give you instant relief, you show a healthy instinct to stop feeling pain. All you need to do is to make more informed choices on how to find long-lasting cures.

At this point, I could try to describe every stress-busting alternative available to you. My list would include well-known techniques like:

- Alexander technique
- Aromatherapy
- Autogenetic therapy
- Bach flower remedies
- Herbalism
- Homoeopathy

- Martial arts
- Massage
- Meditation
- Osteopathy
- Pilates
- Shiatsu
- T'ai chi
- Yoga

I recommend that you take up something along these lines to combat exam stress. Students often find one thing in particular that keeps them going: martial arts, for instance, offer many people the stamina and focus they need in the run-up to their exams.

Is there a breathing meditation I can practise straight away?

Yes. You can do this anywhere, even with your eyes open. It takes 20 minutes and improves concentration, calming the mind.

1 Breathe normally. Just *after* you breathe out, count silently, 'one'. Count 'two' after the second exhalation. Go up to ten. Then start again from one. Do this for five minutes.

   It's quite normal to lose count. When you notice this, start again at one

2 Now make your silent count just *before* you breathe in. Do this for five minutes.
3 Stop counting, and for another five minutes just notice the sensation of breathing in your body.
4 Spend the last five minutes noticing the point at which air enters and exits the body (either your lips or nostrils).

At the very least build a broad foundation for your well-being on the following Five Pillars of Health, and you'll be in good condition for your exams.

1 Everything in moderation – including moderation

In moderation, the damage done by most quick fixes stays within reparable limits – Ecstasy being perhaps one notable exception to this rule. Therefore, the secret of good physical and mental health is to avoid excess.

Although you need to be persistent, I'd rather you didn't become a health freak. In a student environment, you can't be totally disciplined. Just pay attention to how you lead your life most of the time. A healthy lifestyle is one that doesn't take the healthy lifestyle to extremes.

2 Eat well

The benefits of a good diet are often completely underestimated. This is probably because the effects are, for most part, preventative: a good diet contributes to a strong nervous system, immunity against disease, restful sleep and clear thinking.

Make food a priority

The conditions in which you eat your food also matter. Food gulped down in front of the computer is harder to digest. If you can take time to eat your food in a relaxed setting you will extract more nutrients and derive greater benefit from what you eat. You are not just *what* you eat, you are also *how* you eat – so take time off for meals.

5 portions of fruit/veg.

As a broad guideline, your diet should be varied and contain fresh fruit and vegetables (the sooner you eat these after purchasing them, the more vitamins they retain). It's recommended that you eat five portions from either category, every day. In his remarkably comprehensive book, *Healing with Whole Foods: Oriental Traditions and Modern Nutrition*, Paul Pitchford advises that people who tend towards addictive patterns of behaviour with tranquillisers, alcohol or even chocolate should eat magnesium-rich foods – whole grains, beans and pulses, vegetables, seaweeds, nuts and seeds.

Brain foods

These foods are also good for the brain. Nutritionists point out the benefits of B vitamins in combating stress and boosting mental performance. Vitamins A, C and E have anti-oxidant properties and play an important role in maintaining a healthy immune system. Lecithin is thought to enhance memory and concentration. All these are contained in the foods outlined above. Put together, avocados, soya beans and fish are also rich in these elements and make outstandingly good foods if you like them and want some extra brain power.

Vitamin manufacturers encourage us to take these nutrients in supplement form, but it isn't recommended that you take supplements for more than a month at a time, as many health professionals warn that, in the long term, the body grows reliant on them, losing the ability to extract nutrients from food. Supplements also give people false reassurance that they can forget about their diet. In fact, there is no evidence that supplements provide the nutritional power base that a balanced diet can offer.

Nutritional advice is available from the British Nutrition Foundation – see page 203 for their address.

3 Exercise

Exercise: do some!

In my experience, students know the value of exercise, and I shall therefore remain brief on the subject. Suffice it to say that exercise plays a vital part in counterbalancing the stress responses produced in our bodies by having to meet deadlines and exams. Here are five ways in which exercise provides an outlet for the fight or flight response triggered in these conditions:

- Relieves pent-up frustrations from sitting in lectures and tutorials, writing essays and revising for exams.
- Counterbalances a sedentary, intellectual lifestyle.
- Aerobic exercise releases endorphins into the bloodstream, producing a sense of euphoria and promoting relaxation.
- Lowers blood pressure and helps circulation.
- Relaxes tense muscles.

Exercise provides an outlet for pent-up frustrations

4 Sleep

Sleep is such a hugely underrated activity that I shall devote a little more space to it in these pages. Indeed, people sleep about 90 minutes less per night than they did in the nineteenth century, and the rate is falling still. In 1995, a survey by First Direct Bank

Value sleep

found that the average night's sleep lasted seven hours and 12 minutes, 25 minutes less than in 1990. Apart from the electric light-bulb, the culprits seem to be a tendency to undervalue the benefits of sleep and overvalue the benefits of hard work, and a cultural trend towards shift work, especially computer work. Yet, numerous studies show that sleep deprivation impairs mental performance.

Although the hours of sleep before midnight are thought to be the most beneficial, it's common for students to burn the midnight oil, to watch TV or meet social or academic demands. An erratic lifestyle like this commonly produces sleep problems.

If your body clock is deregulated, you may suffer from insomnia, struggling to get to sleep at night, or waking up too early. This can be totally dispiriting when it happens. It's absolutely awful lying in bed at night or early in the morning, fretting about how exhausting the day ahead will be on not enough sleep.

I sleep a lot less now that I'm at university. Will that affect my performance?

Yes. A neuropsychologist at the University of British Columbia, Canada, has measured that losing one hour's sleep out of eight reduces your IQ by one point the next day. Dr Stanly Coren explains: 'For every additional hour lost, you drop two points. And it accumulates. So if you cheat on sleep by two hours a night over a five-day week, you've lost 15 points. If you take the normal run of people – who start with an IQ of 100 – by Friday they're borderline retarded.'

Those with higher IQs are also affected by sleep deprivation: 'Short-term memory goes, along with flexible thinking. You talk in clichés. Nor can you hold complex matters in your head or act on them sensibly. You go on autopilot.'

Regulate yourself

In either case, the problem can often be resolved by going to bed and getting up at regular times, even if you feel exhausted all day: the tiredness you accumulate will produce a good night's sleep thereafter, whereas if you try to compensate for your insomnia by getting up late or taking long afternoon naps, you risk stripping your internal clock of its rhythm, producing a similar effect to jet lag.

Insomnia isn't an illness: it's a symptom. Try to work out what's keeping you awake. You may be stressed because you haven't yet organised your work: maybe a timetable would help you. In addition, the following approaches may help you sleep deeply:

- Wind down at least an hour before you go to bed – watching TV or working on the computer (even just to check emails) can make you too buzzy to go to sleep.
- Avoid tea, coffee and fizzy drinks, and have supper early so that your digestion is well under way before your head hits the pillow.
- Balance your diet: foods rich in B vitamins and calcium aid restful sleep.
- Homoeopathic remedies, Bach flower remedies and aromatherapy work well for different people. Camomile tea is an acquired taste – nice with a slice of lemon (cover it to prevent fumes evaporating away, and don't brew for more than three minutes, or it has a stimulating effect!). Try a few drops of lavender aromatherapy oil on your pillow.
- If your sinuses can tolerate it, you might like some hot milk (no cocoa, because of the caffeine content).
- Hypnotherapy tapes, yoga exercises and breathing meditations (see page 46) can put you in the right frame of mind for sleep.
- Put all your thoughts in an imaginary box. Throw the box into an imaginary sea. Watch it disappear . . .
- Keep a note-pad by the bed: write down your ideas or worries; alternatively, get up and write a letter or diary entry, then go back to bed.
- Listen to music or mindless chatter on the radio.
- Tell yourself *not* to fall asleep: try to lie awake as if you have to get up.
- Tense every muscle in your body; after tensing, relax. Start with your feet and work your way up to your crown.
- Notice if you are fighting sleep: remind yourself how restful it is, or how much you enjoy it, and how wonderful it felt to sleep the night before.
- Early morning insomnia is often cured by eating.

Beat insomnia

Don't struggle or fight it

Even if none of these techniques work for you, remind yourself that just by lying down your body can rest. That awareness takes considerable pressure away. The chances are that you will fall asleep.

5 Express yourself

The way you feel about your work and other issues in your life plays a huge part in how you deal with stress. The first issue worth looking into is your personality type. Research suggests that this plays a major part in determining how well you fare in stressful circumstances. United States cardiologists Meter Friedmann and

Look inwards

Ray Rosenman observed the following traits among their most critical patients, whom they called Type A patients:

Type A personalities are stress-prone

- Pushed for time – rushing to do more in less time.
- Excessively competitive – hostile and aggressive upon slightest provocation.
- Do two or more things at once, at inappropriate times.
- Badly organised – don't plan to achieve necessary goals.

If you recognise yourself in this profile, you might do well to recall the advice in Chapter 1. This will help you develop a more relaxed approach. Practise taking a longer view, setting yourself realistic targets and being forgiving of yourself if you fail to meet your deadlines. Remember to keep disconnecting your self-esteem from your grades.

The second issue has to do with your life experiences. I'm perpetually astonished by the degree to which students underestimate the impact on their lives of traumas such as bereavement, divorce, abuse, bullying, illness or accidents. They imagine that anything that happened in the past can't be relevant today. Time alone has no magic properties: problems that have not been resolved don't simply go away.

Past trauma → present stress

Add the emotional, academic and financial pressures of education at higher levels, and it isn't surprising that the suicide rate among student populations is high: in the UK, about 500 men and 100 women take their lives at university each year. Male students are particularly at risk because they don't talk easily about their problems, particularly their relationship problems, which are the most common cause of suicide. While women are twice as likely to attempt suicide, men are ten times more likely to succeed.

Talk to someone

Let's face it: the student environment isn't conducive to mental health. If you have a problem, I'd urge you to find someone who can listen and maybe even help.

Talk to a friend – or not

Talk to a friend

People often say that a conversation with a friend is as good as therapy. Although I think this seriously undervalues the benefit of therapy, I agree that the compassion that a friend can show just by listening is therapeutic in itself.

However, many students feel, rightly or wrongly, that they can't confide in their friends. They may be reluctant to take up a friend's time, or fear becoming dependent – friendships tend not to work very well where one is constantly propping up the other. They may find that talking to a friend increases their frustration: very few friends listen properly without interrupting to talk about their own problems. Or they may worry that their friends will stop liking them, make judgements, betray confidentiality, or that by talking to them, they betray others.

At particularly low ebbs, students feel they have no friends anyway. Sometimes, this is one of the causes of their depression. Whatever the reason, if you are finding it hard to cope and you don't feel you can talk to a friend, you need another outlet.

Staff

Many staff members care about students' well-being and are willing to help in practical ways: for instance, a tutor might be able to give extra academic support and rearrange a deadline; a nurse may be able to make regular visits. Staff members often have experience and training in dealing with a variety of student problems, from illness to anxiety and depression.

... or a tutor/ nurse

Sometimes, though, students don't want to talk to staff, as they may not wish to confide in anyone connected with their academic life. If the problem is personal, it may be more appropriate to seek more specialist back-up.

Student support services

Thank goodness, colleges and universities are becoming increasingly sensitive to the need for support services. A student at Leicester University, for instance, has access to the following:

- Welfare Service, which gives practical information on financial, health and legal matters and coordinates pastoral care for students living in self-catering accommodation.
- Study Support Centre for students with special needs and disabilities to get support, do their work, rest and socialise.
- Student Learning Centre, which offers study skills advice and gives individual consultations.
- Careers Service.
- English Language Teaching Unit for international students.
- Students' Union.
- Nightline telephone counselling service.

Get support from your establishment

Helplines

Helplines are notoriously underused: an estimated 25 per cent of young people need help and yet only 3 per cent of students use the various counselling and helpline services available to them.

In addition to student helplines, the Samaritans is an organisation of trained volunteers who also deal with student problems. Contrary to popular belief, you don't have to be suicidal to use this service: you can ring about an essay crisis, for instance. I called this organisation after a blistering row, and found it extremely helpful to relate the problem to a complete stranger. The Samaritans also operate an email service (details are given at the back of this book).

Helplines are underused

The advantage of helplines is that the people who run them have training and experience; they can usually refer you to services in your area where you can get regular support. Of course, student helplines and other such services have their limitations, since they can't provide the more sustained and skilled degree of support that counselling or psychotherapy services can offer.

Counselling

Most colleges and universities now offer free student counselling, or you may have access to psychotherapy services offered by the National Health Service (NHS) (talk to your doctor). Despite the availability of these therapies, students can be very nervous about seeking professional help, often because they fear being classified as mentally ill. Yet, counsellors and psychotherapists are not psychiatrists: they have no medical training or prescriptive powers. Theirs is simply a talking cure which works by clarifying goals and drawing out unconscious processes that obstruct progress. They also provide sustained emotional support through difficult times. If you need it, talking to a specialist can help you effect change on a deeper level than is possible simply by reading this book.

The differences between counselling and psychotherapy are largely to do with the level of training the professional has received. A bereavement counsellor, for instance, can start work after a few months' training; a student counsellor should have a minimum of two years' training, preferably accredited by the British Association for Counselling; psychotherapy training takes a minimum of three years. You're entitled to ask what training your counsellor or psychotherapist has received.

One problem that sometimes arises is that the student seeking counselling outwits the counsellor. However, everyone that I know who has had successful counselling or psychotherapy has a story to tell about one professional who wasn't up to scratch. You too may come across counsellors and psychotherapists who aren't very good – keep looking.

In addition to your gut feeling, the following pointers might help you see whether you're in good hands. A good counsellor:

- Steers clear of giving advice, even if you beg for it. The best advice is the advice you give yourself, once you understand what it is that you want.
- Doesn't check up on your progress or direct you, but helps you to come to understandings so that you can direct yourself. If someone asks whether you tidied up your room, as you said you would, that person is taking on a parental role, not a counselling one.

Good counselling clarifies your goals

- Keeps good time, so that you know exactly how long you have, and sessions end punctually.
- Doesn't praise or blame. The purpose of therapy is to help you develop your own thoughts, not seek someone else's approval.
- Doesn't chat during sessions, and allows necessary silences.
- Never makes you do anything you don't want to do.
- Doesn't talk about his or her own life, even if you ask. The sessions are about you, not anyone else.
- Keeps a professional distance. There's no chance of socialising, even though you discuss personal issues in your sessions.

Note that such rules can occasionally be broken, provided this is done in the right spirit.

To help demystify how counselling works, the cartoon at the end of this chapter illustrates a typical revelation in a student counselling session.

A note . . .

By distinguishing between these Five Pillars, I may give the impression that they are somehow independent of each other. They're all intimately connected. For example, a deficient diet will inhibit sleep, whereas exercise will aid it; the quality of your sleep will in turn have a knock-on effect on your psychological welfare, which, of course, affects sleep. The Five Pillars represent a matrix of elements towards which you need to develop a holistic and sustained approach. Do that, and you'll be laughing.

The Five Pillars are interdependent

In a nutshell

In a student setting, the chances are that you will be tempted to deal with academic challenges by using quick fixes. However, a fix that works fast is likely to burn up all your energy in one go, leaving you devitalised, and sending you back to square one – or even further back than that. Once in a while, that's fine, and your system can recover. Over time, however, imbalances build up. You may not perceive their effect in your twenties, but illnesses bred early in adulthood tend to hit people in mid-life, by which time it can be very hard to make lifestyle changes. Fortunately, there are plenty of alternatives to quick fixes.

Your studies are important, but never at the cost of your physical and mental well-being. Besides, if you are well, you will perform better in exams. Exams offer you an opportunity to practise facing challenges by building up your strengths, so that when the deadline comes, you meet it alive and kicking.

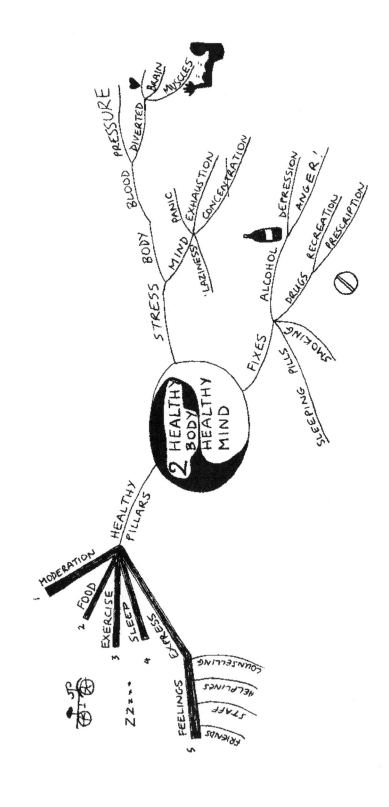

Part II

Techniques for success

3

Lay solid study foundations

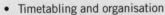

- Timetabling and organisation
- Tackling procrastination
- The value of time off
- Effective work patterns

I like work: I think it's fascinating. I can sit and stare at it for hours.
Jerome K. Jerome

*Exam success
=
emotional
resilience +
study skills*

In dealing with the onset of coursework and exams, students need two crucial inner strengths. The first, as I think you probably realise by now, is resilience – the mental and physical capacity to overcome the frustrations and anxieties that inevitably arise when facing exams. Chapters 1 and 2 offer new ways of thinking (and feeling) about your studies, solutions that I hope you'll find helpful from now on.

Obviously, students' capacity to perform also depends on their degree of academic mastery. Much rests on how effectively you use your study time, on the quality of your approach to your coursework and on your revision and exam technique. Broadly speaking, the rest of this book helps you consolidate all of these study skills.

This particular chapter helps you get the most out of the time and effort you put into your work. It also offers solutions to typical problems students have in organising their learning, particularly in getting started. Learning isn't always fun: even those on courses they adore sometimes find the material difficult, boring, pointless or overwhelming.

People are
more capable
than they think

Without method, students can easily grow despondent about their work, particularly in cases where there is some real or imagined cause for worry. This may be a history of underperforming at school, past failure or a long absence from studying – as is the case with many mature students. Alternatively, it may be an educational 'diagnosis', which could be just one comment by an influential teacher or parent that they are incompetent, to a full-blown dyslexia report. It doesn't take much for people to convince themselves that they aren't as capable as the others on their course.

Good study
habits draw out
your strengths

Yet, even people with a diagnosed learning difficulty such as dyslexia or dyspraxia can compete if they have good study techniques (see Appendix 4).

A clearer understanding of how to learn can help enormously. Therefore, not only will the ideas in this chapter enable your coursework and exam preparation to run smoothly, they will also brighten up the way you feel about your work. And if you recognise yourself in the case study below, you certainly need that.

Do you recognise Dan?

Dan has revision to do. He meant to start it weeks ago, but has (typically) kept putting it off. His deadline is very close now, so he is quite anxious to get going.

He starts at 5 p.m. First, it takes him an hour to collect all his materials, because he can't remember where he put his notes. By the time all his equipment is ready – pens, paper, books and files neatly arranged – he feels ravenous. A quick trip to a local take-away, and he jumps back to his desk by . . . oh, 6.45.

As 6.45 is no time to start anything, he waits for a nice round figure (7.00) and then starts on page 1, line 1 of his notes. At 7.10 he casually flicks through his file and sees with horror that he has another 24 pages to go. As he calculates how long this will take, he escapes into a daydream that lasts 10 wonderful minutes. At 7.20 he realises he is wasting time, and the guilt makes him feel bad, so he stares glumly at his work for the next half hour. He doesn't take anything in and the words on the page swim before his eyes.

Dan
procrastinates
– why?

You get the picture. Dan spends all evening on what could be done in one hour. He stops, eventually, not because his work is finished, but because he feels tired and fed up, and can't stand the topic any more.

For argument's sake, let's keep his problems simple. Let's say he hasn't got a hangover, his parents aren't divorced, he has a delightful relationship and the family dog is still alive. Why, then, should he be struggling with his work?

First, if you've read Chapter 1 you'll have spotted that Dan ① *Low self-esteem* suffers from a basic problem with his self-esteem. Consciously, he hopes to do some work; unconsciously, his task is a chance to confirm how incapable he thinks he is. There's a voice in his head, of which he is probably totally unaware, which goes something like, 'This is going to take me ages. I'm a loser, so I can't really do this. Others could. Not me.'

As outlined in Part I, thoughts like this can be brought to the surface through discussions with others or in counselling. In the *(a common ailment)* open, they are easily challenged. But it's remarkable how many students like Dan carry a total conviction that they are inferior to others. Little do they realise that everyone else is affected by much the same belief.

The second reason why Dan struggles with his work is that he ② *No strategies* needs to be more strategic. He tries, but because he makes the wrong kind of effort, he gets tired, gives up and simply reinforces his belief that he is no good.

> **I feel useless: everyone else seems to manage except me. What's wrong with me?**
>
> Nothing. Comedian Richard Herring has a degree in history from Oxford University, yet, like many students, he felt academically inferior throughout his university life. 'Everything was made extra nerve-racking because there was an exam at the end of the first term. I imagined that I'd fail, that everyone would find out that I'd got in by some fluke and I would be thrown out . . . I didn't have any idea whether I was good or not.' His final 2:1 came as a shock.
>
> His advice for university students? 'Don't feel intimidated – everyone feels the same.'

Organise your time

The most helpful strategy Dan could adopt is to set time limits. In the *short term*, this would give him an idea of when his work would finish. As it is, he simply gives himself all evening. This is very inefficient.

Dan's first need: a timetable

Time limits would also help him complete his *long-term* tasks in good time. Left to his own devices, he wastes precious weeks (his procrastination is understandable, given that he finds working so difficult). A timetable would be a good start.

Timetabling means facing the monster

Many students resist drawing up timetables. Timetabling means facing the monster: working out a comprehensive list of everything you have to do and the time you have to do it. This can be a daunting prospect.

A good timetable includes time off

Fortunately, a monster you face is never quite as scary as one you don't. Once you've looked at your tasks, and broken them down into manageable chunks, you'll realise you have work to do – sure – but you'll also see that you have plenty of free time. In fact, any self-respecting timetable should include time off.

This makes the prospect of working considerably easier to handle.

Face that scary timetabling monster

Week	Mon	Tues	Wed	Thur	Fri	Sat	Sun
1			Finish researching essay 1			Off	
2	Finish researching essay 2		Finish planning proposal 1			Off	Finish planning proposal 2
3	Supervisor				Finish altering proposals 1 and 2	Off	
4			Finish essay 1			Off	
5						Off	Finish essay 2
6		Re-read essays and finish final touches			Hand in essays 1 and 2	Off	

Timetabling gives you margin for error . . .
to include a bibliography and make corrections to layout, pagination, cover sheets, and so on. Sod's law guarantees that these tedious tasks take as long as the essay itself (the bibliography requires extra research, your layout goes awry, the printer runs out of ink . . .).

- Between finishing both essays and handing them in, there is a two-day safety margin.

Of course, you may have other deadlines, such as term essays and modular exams. You want to avoid having to do everything in the same weeks. At higher levels, there's a strong chance that *. . . and helps spread tasks* this may happen, since tutors rarely consult with each other when setting essays, so you can suddenly get two essays in a week. Therefore, it makes sense to put your calendar together as early as you can, so that you spread all these different tasks through the term. That way, your coursework and revision are catered for despite other demands on your time.

The second function of timetabling is to take a short-term view *Timetable the short-term* and organise a daily schedule. Your aim is to plan the detail of your activities. To do this some students adopt a Filofax-style approach.

Others just want a rough idea of what needs to be done – they'll decide how to do it when the time comes. The following two diary extracts show you two very different students' approach to time-tabling. Both have the following agendas:

- Attend one tutorial
- Attend one lecture
- Revise last week's notes
- Finish off a piece of coursework which involves some background research

Jack's timetable

Day	a.m.		p.m.		eve.	
Mon	10.00	Library, to read coursework source material	1.00 2.00 3.30 3.45 4.15 5.15	Lunch Tutorial Revise last week's notes Tea Plan coursework Stop		Pub
Tues	10.30 12.00 12.15	Lecture Break Write up coursework	1.00	Lunch Afternoon off	7.00 8.00 10.45	Dinner Write up coursework Stop

As you can see, Jack likes to be exact. He gets a sense of achievement from sticking as closely to his timetable as possible, and he has incorporated enough time off in his routine to ensure that his work stays within reasonable limits and that he can fulfil his goals.

Having said that, this routine is so regimented that it's best if Jack only sets himself such goals at critical points rather than on a daily basis. He also risks being disappointed if, as is very likely, *Regimented...* he fails to stay exactly on schedule. Jack's timetable is fine as long as he realises this is just a model for him to follow, one which will require making adjustments through the day, to make way for the unexpected – the unexpected being, after all, the spice of life.

Chloe's timetable

Mon	Events	Tutorial (2 p.m.) Party (7 p.m.)
	To do	Library, for coursework research (3 hours) Plan coursework (1 hour) Revise last week's notes (15 mins)
Tues	Events	Lecture (10.30 a.m.)
	To do	Write essay (3–4 hours)

. . . vs loose

Unlike Jack, Chloe doesn't like to be regimented. She doesn't go into details, as she prefers a looser structure to her day. This approach suits her, as she tends not to leave her work till the last minute. She likes to have an idea of what she will do and how long it will take. However, she doesn't like pinning herself down to particular times. She knows she has to go to the library on Monday, but she won't decide until Monday morning whether she goes before or after her tutorial – it depends on how she feels when she wakes up. Chloe is more flexible than Jack, which is fine as long as she remains realistic about how much she can achieve in the time available.

Ten tips on how to fail at timetabling

By now, you're probably sick of being told how to organise your time productively. So here's refreshing advice on how to make your timekeeping an unmitigated disaster:

1 Make your timetable a punishing one. Plan to work hours you've never worked in your life. This will make you hate your routine and, if you have any sense, you'll quickly give it up.

Tried & tested ways to sabotage timetabling

2 Give yourself absolutely no margin before your deadlines, so that you are completely caught out if the unexpected happens and you get ill or have a bust-up with your best friend. This also means that however lovely the weather, you'll be stuck at your desk, which will have the same effect on your spirits as item 1 above.

3 Plan to work every day in the week. Afternoons off are a definite no-no. By working non-stop, you make it extremely hard to gain a sense of overview or to absorb new ideas. This will convince you that you have to work non-stop. Neat, isn't it?

4 Aim to work no less than five hours a day. In fact, why not plan to work all day? A limit on the hours you work each day could make you dangerously efficient.

5 When you schedule in revision for more than one topic, you can organise yourself in various ways. To focus on one thing at a time you can timetable a block of revision per topic. For more variety in your revision, you can do one topic in the morning and another in the afternoon. Whatever you do, choose the option you most dislike, and be sure to timetable your most difficult topics back-to-back, so that you stand little chance of seeing your revision through to the end.

6 Research suggests that the type of work you do in the morning sets you up for the rest of the day. You can use this to your advantage: by doing filing every morning, you successfully dull your mind for the afternoon.

7 Spend time on big jobs first, so as not to have time for little jobs that might be over quickly.

8 If you're the type who gets carried away, you're in a perfect position to timetable revision for your final exam last. Timetabling for your final exam *first* might help you prepare for it in good time. Such foresight must be avoided at all costs. (Apply this principle for coursework essays too.)

9 Give up on your timetable the minute you fall behind. Under no circumstances should you attempt to revise it. If it doesn't work perfectly first time round, it's a lousy idea and you're better off leaving everything to chance.

10 Draw up your timetable on your own. Don't get anyone to help you – they might suggest ways of making it realistic, and then you'd have to admit that timetabling does work.

I've tried but I can't stick to a timetable. What's the alternative?

A system of daily time quotas might suit you better: just set yourself a minimum (but realistic) number of hours' revision per day. If you work over the minimum, you can have time off the next day; if you work under the minimum, you have to make up the time. You can reassess your quotas each week.

A word about organisation

Back to Dan. If you recall, he couldn't remember where he put his notes, so he wasted an hour looking for them. You can save a lot of time by being systematic about where you keep papers.

Organise papers using a drawer . . .

I have a middle drawer into which I shove all tasks that I need to do and all tasks I'm currently doing, because I hate having my working surfaces cluttered up with irritating bits of paper. Everything goes by topic into plastic files. Pressing tasks stay on my desk or go to the top of my drawer, loose-leaf. When my drawer starts to overflow, I have a clear-out and file away what's finished.

. . . or two trays

Other people use trays. The principle is the same. You have two trays: one for things that need doing, and another for things that are done and need to be sent out or filed. This saves hunting down precious papers, since they can only ever be in a tray or a file.

Keep 'To Do' lists

When you have a task to do, make a note of it *immediately* so that you have a written reminder. It's exhausting and risky trying to hold everything in your head. Write your 'To Do' lists in the same book or computer file; if you use scraps of paper, put all your scraps in one designated place. (I often scribble messages to myself on my page-a-day desk calendar, since it's always at hand.) Arrange your lists in order of priority.

TO DO

α — ~~finish CW essay~~ —

β Plan essay 2

α Read last chapter of B.

γ Library : return books

α Phone mum

β Mindmap for RV of psychoanalytic themes

α = urgent
β = less urgent
γ = not at all urgent

Arrange your 'To Do' lists in order of priority

Tidying vs procrastination

Note that I haven't mentioned anything about tidying your room, or the contents of your files, or your computer disks. Feng shui warns us that accumulating clutter contributes to a cluttered mind. That's true. But before you rush to clear up the mess, do consider the law which states that the more you tidy, the less you find. Moreover, the 'I'm going to organise all my notes' approach is a well-known technique for avoiding getting started.

Get started

Let's say you've drawn up your timetable and you've prioritised your lists. It's time to do some work. Where do you start?

Overview your work

Look back at poor Dan if you want an example of where not to start: page 1 line 1 of your notes. This laborious approach always spells trouble. Instead, start by overviewing your work. Here's a useful procedure:

Get started by overviewing + setting deadlines

1 Look over your task, to picture what it involves.
2 If it's a simple writing task, decide on a reasonable completion time (you may already have scheduled this into your timetable).
3 If your task involves background research, *draw up what you already know*. This will show you the gaps in your knowledge, saving you going over source material that you already know well enough.
4 Get hold of the right sources of information to help you fill gaps in your knowledge. Working from a good textbook or a good set of notes saves precious time and effort. If you're not sure you have the right background material, ask people around you, even if it means leaving your desk and making a few calls.
5 Looking over your source material, estimate how long it's reasonable to spend on your background research. Be particularly stringent about this if you are doing research using the Internet, as the temptation to find out extraneous information with this medium can be very strong unless you have a clear purpose.
6 Plan regular breaks – more on this later.

> ### Should I work with the computer or on paper?
>
> For coursework, use a computer to do your writing but plan on paper first. Try not to keep editing as you write: make your corrections later so that you don't keep interrupting yourself. Ideally, leave your work for a day or two before you start fiddling with cut and paste options.
>
> Unless you can use your computer in the exam, go back to pen and paper when practising exam-style essays.
>
> For time-saving computer tips, see Appendix 2.

Deadlines are your friend!

By deciding on reasonable completion times in this way, you create little deadlines for yourself. Don't fear deadlines: they're your best friend. At higher levels of education, the work you do could take years. Good studying is about setting reasonable limits – in other words, having a stop time before you even start.

This can really get you cracking, because a stop time impresses upon you that you haven't got all day. Knowing that your time is restricted also forces you to make choices: you have to be strategic, to discriminate between work that's useful to you and work that's not.

A little negotiation does wonders

Overcome resistance to getting started

Even with all these techniques, starting can still be the hardest part. I'm sure you're familiar with those times when you really don't want make the effort to start because you feel tired, bored, distracted, upset, angry or confused. Under such circumstances, it can be hard to resist the temptation to put off working until another time.

Before you succumb to such temptation, try the following strategy. It involves negotiating with the child in you, that part of your personality addicted to instant gratification. Remember the parent–child–adult model explained in Chapter 1? Develop your adult voice:

Child: I want to put this off till tomorrow. I really don't want to do it now.

Adult: I wonder if the reason why you don't want to work today is that you're not in the mood? Maybe you could get in the mood by doing a little. Perhaps you just can't bear working for very long?

Child: Exactly. This work is going to take ages.

Adult: Well, in that case, why don't you work for as long as you can bear – just to get started. Then you can take a quick break and see how you feel about carrying on.

Child: I could do ten minutes. No more, mind.

Adult: Fine. Ten minutes, then you'll take a quick break.

Child: Promise?

Just do ten minutes

Make sure you stop even if you feel like carrying on once your ten minutes are up. (Why? Simply because unless you keep your promise, the deal will never work a second time, as anyone who has spent time with children will confirm.)

After your break, ask yourself whether you want to get back to your work. You can negotiate all over again, if you like.

Why procrastinate?

If that fails, it's worth looking at reasons why you might be tempted to procrastinate. I suggest you jot down the advantages – yes, *advantages* – of leaving your work until the last minute. Here is a space for you to write your ideas:

What I get out of procrastination . . .

Couldn't think of anything? I've met countless students who berate themselves for putting off their work, telling me how stressful it is and how it damages their coursework and exam prospects. Yet, they all agree when I offer a few reasons why they might be choosing the eleventh hour approach:

Procrastination has many benefits!

- It gives you time off now.
- It gives a sense of urgency which lends impetus to the work, particularly for students who are uninterested in their subject.
- It's rebellious: passing exams involves complying with many institutional rules, and therefore it can be satisfying to kick against the system.

- It involves working intensely, which gives a sense of accomplishment.
- Guarding against the risk that work might fill up all time available, it guarantees freedom up to the eleventh hour.
- It's simple to organise: between the eleventh hour and the twelfth, life consists only of work.
- Memorising information over just a short period before an exam dispenses with the need for regular revision.
- It covers your tracks in case you do poorly in the exam – you can tell yourself and everyone else you didn't work (in other words, you reassure everyone that your failure isn't due to stupidity).
- Last-minute cramming is a dramatic, Herculean, high-risk option, so you use exams to boost a frail ego, or prove something to yourself.

Understanding procrastination releases blocks

You may have thought up more reasons. Whatever these are, they're safer out in the open than lurking in the recesses of your unconscious mind. Once you understand why you resist studying, you can condemn yourself a little less, and understand yourself a little more. That makes it easier to work.

Having these reasons out in the open also gives you a chance to challenge them. For instance, it's possible that procrastination is a redundant activity to you now that you have left school and are pursuing your education out of choice, not imposition. Or maybe you feel you *have* no choice, and that's precisely the problem. Maybe something needs to be changed before you can feel free in your work.

Academic/ emotional blocks

If your organisation is very chaotic, some underlying issue is likely to be blocking your progress. This may be an academic difficulty, such as not knowing how to go about your work, in which case this book should help – or ask a tutor. If you think it's an emotional issue, such as a fear of failure (or success) so great that it paralyses you, try talking to someone about it.

Everyone deserves breaks

Let's return to Dan one last time. Notice that he doesn't take breaks. 'No way,' I hear you shout. 'He's lazy enough as it is. He doesn't deserve any.'

Dan's second need: breaks

This, of course, is precisely what Dan believes too. Like most students who have difficulty concentrating on their work, Dan feels he isn't trying hard enough. This is largely because he bathes in a culture dominated by a puritanical ethic (explained in Chapter 1) that *good* work is uninterrupted *hard* work. Proper students, it is thought, never disconnect their eyes from the page.

Breaks aren't highly valued

To make matters worse, in today's world, the all-pervasive 'Don't just sit there, do something' work ethic creates generations of workaholics who feel guilty about taking breaks throughout their lives, from their schooldays to their retirement years. In the new American-style culture that is now fast becoming ours, office workers try to earn brownie points by eating lunch at their desks and doing regular overtime, despite the considerable cost to their health and personal lives.

Breaks are increasingly viewed as a reward for good work, one that has to be earned. Playtime is all but disappearing from our schools. Children are often made to work during their breaks to catch up on work they failed to complete. This punitive approach teaches all children (even those who succeed in completing their work on time) that they don't deserve breaks unless they've worked well in the first place.

It's nonsense.

Ten reasons to take breaks

Here are ten reasons why breaks make students work better:

Breaks are essential

1 Breaks make learning pleasant. It's relatively easy to contemplate settling down to work when you know it will be punctuated by regular interruptions. This enables you to work regularly, as it gives you less reason to delay working.
2 Breaks maintain concentration over time. By taking breaks even when you're not tired, you take preventative action.
3 Breaks refresh your mind, giving you a better overview of your work.
4 Breaks create deadlines. As I've explained, deadlines help you knuckle down.
5 Studies show that students find it easiest to absorb material at the beginning and the end of their learning periods. Breaks create more beginnings and endings.
6 Breaks need to be planned. You'll find yourself prioritising certain tasks, as you develop a better understanding of how much work you can do in the time available.
7 Breaks teach self-control: you have to learn to stop and start.
8 Breaks help learning and offer fresh insights, because we absorb information and make links during breaks. Unconscious activity of this kind is manifest every time you try in vain to

remember someone's name or some other detail, only for it to pop into your head just as you give up.

9 Breaks create an opportunity to revise. After your break, it's useful to recap earlier material.

10 Your eyesight will suffer if you don't take your eyes off the page or computer screen. Breaks are good for your body.

I know, but please don't make *me* take a break!

Despite knowing all these reasons to take breaks, you may still find it hard to incorporate them in your study routine.

Breaks encourage discipline

Part of the trouble is that freedom is thought to be an easy thing. In fact, it's hard: you'll need to practise using your free time well if you have no training in this particular art. Children are usually so regimented that they go wild in their time off, which, sadly, reinforces the view that their free time should be restricted and organised. The consequence is that few young adults know how to use their leisure productively. Give them 10 minutes off, and they will usually make a beeline for the television, which is just another way of being organised by some outside force.

This is one reason why many students resist taking breaks: they fear being unable to control their freedom. Yet, with a little thought you could learn to discipline yourself.

Organise your pastimes

It's usually helpful to make some decisions before you take a break, such as how long you think it should be, and what you want to do in that time. Obviously, do whatever you enjoy, bearing in mind that activities best avoided at break time are things like:

Avoid activities that get out of hand

- A quick sleep
- Just one go at the computer game
- A pint or two
- A kitchen spree, if you're a gourmet
- A music session, if you're a part-time disc-jockey

Refresh yourself

Activities like watching TV or surfing the net resemble very closely the work you do as you study, particularly as they involve gazing at a TV or computer screen. On the other hand, any physical exercise you can do in your break is helpful, getting you back in touch with your body.

If you're a smoker, think about alternating smoking with other pastimes if you don't want to end up having a cigarette every break. You may recall from Chapter 2 that caffeine-rich substances such as cola drinks, tea, coffee and chocolate will also make you tense and jittery. Not only are all these substances unhealthy in large doses, but the effect they have on your nerves makes it extremely hard to sit still and concentrate.

How can I stop straining my eyes at the computer?

Do some palming for a few minutes: cup the palms of your hands over your eyes so that you cut out all light (but don't press on your eyelids). Your eyes will be soothed and refreshed by the darkness and warmth. You can visualise pleasant scenes if you like.

This technique helps to preserve your vision. It's also good for headaches.

Take a break at an interesting point

Returning to work after breaks can still be tricky. You may do all the right things during your breaks, yet still find it hard to get back to your work. If so, try *stopping at interesting or incomplete points in your work.*

You may protest: 'When I'm focused on something, there's no way I can interrupt myself. I need to carry on.' You may be right. On the other hand, it's possible that your impulse to finish what you do comes from having been told, when you were little, 'Make sure you finish that first, before you have your tea.' In those days,

Break at interesting points

your workload was smaller. All that has changed now. If you wait until your work is finished before you leave your desk, you risk going on for hours. That's not good for your concentration or your morale.

Roald Dahl used to make himself stop when he least wanted to, to ensure he was always eager to return to his desk and finish off his cliffhanger. It stopped him getting writer's block. If it was good enough for him . . .

Break as often as you like

How often you break depends largely on your personality, the work you're doing and your mood. Some people like to programme their breaks into their watches. Others find it irritating to work under constant timed conditions.

The more you have to learn, the more you need breaks

When revising – in other words, trying to absorb a mass of information – it's best to take short, frequent breaks, and to avoid working for more than 40 minutes at one time. If your revision is heavy going, you can stay fresh and alert for long stints by taking a five-minute break every 20 minutes. After your break, recap previous material for a minute or two, and then repeat the cycle.

When you're engaged in more creative pursuits, such as essay writing and coursework, try not to work more than an hour without stopping. Because I tend to get carried away and forget the time when I'm writing, I sometimes set an alarm to ensure I don't go over the hour.

You can also schedule your timetable around long breaks. If you refer back to Jack's timetable on page 68, you'll observe that he never works for very long without stopping for lunch, tea or dinner.

Put theory into practice . . . your way

Don't nag yourself

Good study habits can sometimes take time to perfect, as there may be complex reasons why you can't carry them out with instant success. Notice if taking time off makes you feel guilty: if so, you are suffering from the puritanical work ethic. Try to pinpoint whose voice it is that's nagging you. If you realise you have internalised the voice of a parent or a teacher, you may be able to detach from it.

Find your own routine

It takes about seven repetitions for an action to become a habit. So persevere! These principles are there to guide you but apply them with flexibility and develop, where you see fit, your own individual approach. With a little persistence, you'll find that your learning really starts to improve.

In a nutshell

Take your free time as seriously as you do your work. This will help you work regularly and willingly. Organise your work in a way that works for you – work patterns are very individual: there's no point in trying to conform to someone else's idea of how you should be organising yourself.

The coursework and exam checklist in Appendix 1 may also help you keep a firm grip on your preparation and revision.

I will close this chapter with the encouraging words of Mark Twain, a productive man if ever there was:

'The secret of getting ahead is getting started. The secret of getting started is breaking your complex overwhelming tasks into small manageable ones, and then starting on the first one.'

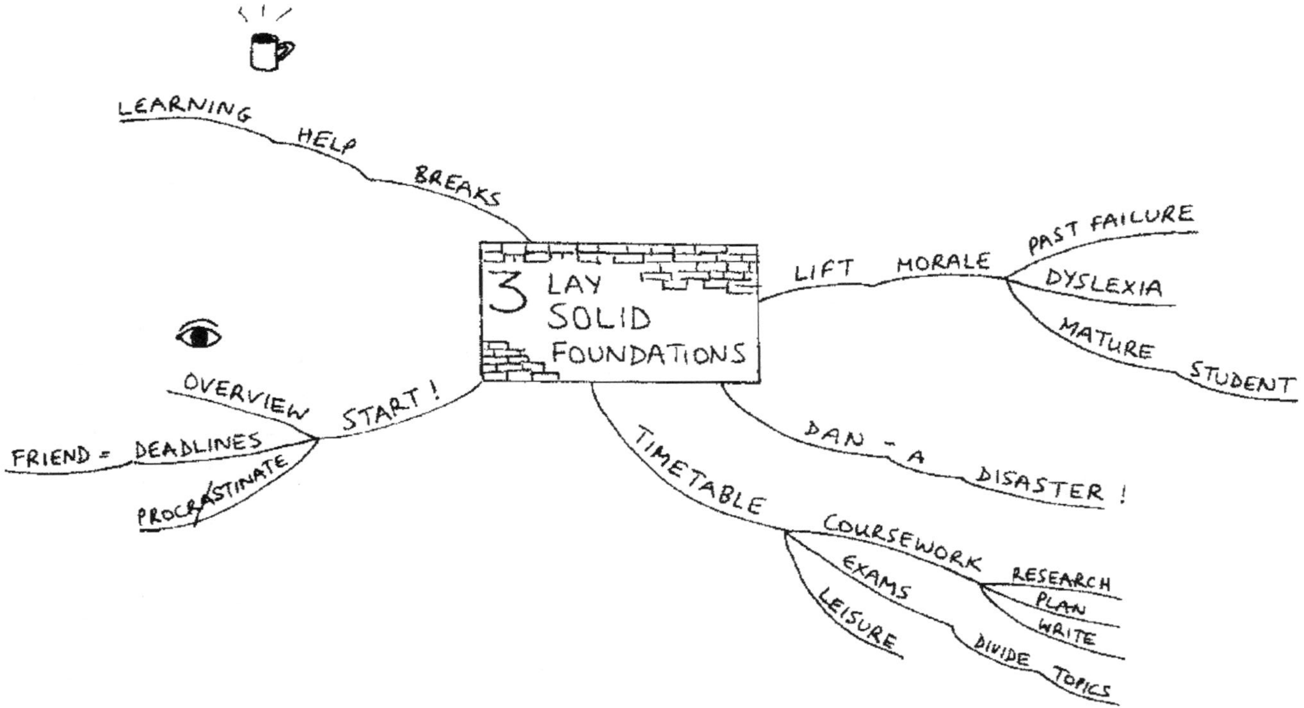
3 LAY SOLID FOUNDATIONS
LIFT MORALE
PAST FAILURE
DYSLEXIA
MATURE STUDENT
DAN - A DISASTER !
TIMETABLE
COURSEWORK
RESEARCH
PLAN
WRITE
EXAMS
DIVIDE TOPICS
LEISURE
START !
OVERVIEW
DEADLINES
FRIEND =
PROCRASTINATE
BREAKS
HELP
LEARNING

4

Remember, remember

- Memory explained
- Active versus passive learning
- Mindmaps
- Memory tricks

I remember leaves
Green as spearmint, crisp as paper
I remember trees
Bare as coat racks, spread like broken umbrellas

Stephen Sondheim

Now that you're finding it easier to get down to work, let's ease your burden further and help you use your memory.

The greatest fear students have is that they have too much to remember, and that this memory overload will make them go *Memory can be* blank in the exam. Yet, good recall isn't just a static, genetic thing: *improved* you can improve your memory quite easily, rather as you would train a muscle. When I was preparing for my own finals, I learnt to use my memory so well, using the techniques outlined in this chapter, that I became able to remember sequences of numbers instantly. Far from weakening it, you too will find that exercising your memory in the ways suggested here will make it stronger and stronger.

All you have to do is to learn how to use this extraordinary tool.

Understand your memory

Do you understand how your memory works? Unless you do, it's quite unsettling to observe that you remember things on some occasions and then, without apparent reason, forget them on others.

People don't realise why recall fails

For example, let's say you need to learn a poem for a Monday afternoon presentation. If your presentation makes the grade, you will be performing it in front of an audience on Friday. You learn it on Sunday afternoon. Come Sunday evening, you can barely recall a word, so you prepare yourself for disappointment on Monday. Come Monday, however, you find you can recite it expertly. You are a little surprised, since your recall was so poor the night before. You are through to the Friday performance. Confident that you know the poem, since you recited it so well on Monday, you don't go over it again. On Friday morning, you realise you have forgotten the poem.

In other words, on the day of learning, you forget; the day after, you remember; but then a few days after that, you forget again. Why does your memory fluctuate so dramatically over one week?

Sleep helps you learn

The answer is simple, but startling. Recall *improves* after the first night's sleep. After that, as you would expect, it starts to deteriorate.

The reason why you remember something better after sleeping on it is that sleep is a rather mysterious and magical process that enables our minds to absorb the day's information and link it to other experiences.

Here's the scientific backup, if you're interested.

Recall improves on a night's sleep

Electro-encephalograph (EEG) research shows that there are two types of sleep. Slow-wave deep sleep (SWS) mostly occurs in the first half of the night. It alternates with periods of rapid-eye movement (REM) sleep, which occur when we dream. Our brains contain two memory centres: the hippocampus, which stores explicit, high-impact information – such as what happened today – and the cortex, which absorbs deeper levels of information. Both are active and communicate with each other during sleep. Position emission tomography (PET) scans show that in SWS, nerve cells fire off along a neural channel from the hippocampus to the cortex, as if to tell the cortex what happened today. During REM, they fire back to the hippocampus, as if the cortex was replying, deepening the understanding by looking at everything in relation

Nightly communications between your two memory centres consolidate learning

to everything else, making creative links. This flow of information to and from both memory centres enables information to be integrated meaningfully overnight.

And so we say: *the morning is wiser than the evening.* According to research conducted in the 1990s at Harvard Medical School in the USA, the morning is in fact 24 per cent wiser, on average. Students who were given tests to practise performed better after a night's sleep. Results were proportional to the amount of SWS and REM sleep students had in the first and last quarter of the night respectively. Some students, whose performance improved by as much as 40 per cent, didn't like the idea that their progress was due to good sleep. They preferred to think they performed better because they were more intelligent. I told you in Chapter 2 that the benefits of sleep are completely underestimated, didn't I?

The conclusion is this: sleep helps you learn. Anything you cover today, you will remember and understand significantly better tomorrow – though you may not have been conscious of this until now.

Things make more sense after 24 hours . . . You've probably already experienced this phenomenon in certain contexts. For instance, take a film you saw which had a complicated plot; *The Usual Suspects*, say. At the end of the film, as the credits went up, you were probably dazed and confused. The next day, however, you probably found yourself recalling scenes, and getting flashes of understanding. Your unconscious mind started to make links.

The fact that a night's sleep does wonders for recall explains why countless schoolchildren put off learning until 24 hours before a test. Although they and their parents might talk of laziness and procrastination, and say they wish the preparation had started well before that time, this strategy – for it is a strategy – produces such excellent results that they usually repeat the exact same pattern for each test. These children start to worry that they will never find the motivation to prepare anything in good time, since ultimately their procrastination bears surprisingly good fruit.

. . . so it's tempting to learn the night before

In higher education, of course, the eleventh-hour approach is an appalling strategy, given the depth of enquiry required. The earlier you can start learning material, the more margin you give yourself to absorb it and link it to other ideas on your course.

Should I play revision tapes in my sleep? I've heard that can help me learn.

No. Get some proper sleep. Do your learning when you're awake. Sleep will help you to process that information on a deeper level.

Revise at strategic points

Given the way that your memory works, the most effective strategy is to revise the day after you learn something. At that point you have very little re-learning to do, because your recall is at a 'high'.

After that first revision, you still need to revise again, again and again. I'm sorry to say that our memories crave considerable repetition. That's because after the initial memory 'high' that a night's sleep produces, recall starts to deteriorate – and fast.

But don't despair. The 'Five-minute revise guide' overleaf offers you points for optimum revision, thereby reducing the time you spend on each revision to minutes rather than hours.

Try it.

Five-minute revise guide:

1 Revise the day after learning something (when it's fresh in your mind).
2 Revise it again a week later.
3 One month after that second revision, revise for a third time.
4 A fourth and final revision after a term should ensure that the knowledge you have acquired stays permanently lodged in your mind.

Each revision takes about five minutes.

4 optimum
revision times

The practice is simpler than the theory

You may be wondering what student is so organised that he or she revises every single bit of learning after a day, a week, a month and a term. Thankfully, you don't need to be a timetabling guru to implement this revision schedule. Just use this theory as a guideline. For instance, when your files are out, see if you can run certain pages through your mind. It doesn't matter if you're a day late for your first revision, a week late for your second, or a month early for your third. The main thing is to realise that you don't learn material simply by learning it once. It needs to be revised again, again, again and again, at ever-increasing intervals of time.

Easy to
implement

I have to work to music or I can't concentrate. Why's that?

The best explanation I've ever heard on this modern phenomenon comes from Richard DeGrandpre, author of *Ritalin Nation*. In order to focus, your mind needs a certain level of stimulation. But the mind, being a highly adaptive tool, has adapted to today's rapid-fire culture by growing used to high levels of stimulation. A book or a page of notes can't stimulate you as much as TV, radio or computers, and so may not be enough to satisfy your ever-inflated sensory needs. Hence, many students find they have to plug themselves into their stereos before they can pay attention to their work.

Keep the noise to background level so that you're not listening to the tracks, and try to wean yourself off it, as you're much more likely to do good work in comparative silence.

★ Learn actively

By what method do you revise? Do you re-read your notes? Do you learn them by covering up the page and testing yourself? Do you copy things out in neat?

To help you discriminate between useful and useless approaches, you need to spot the difference between the following two types of revision:

Active vs passive learning

1 *Passive revision.* This involves taking information in without attempting to reproduce it. It will always let you down.
2 *Active revision.* This involves reproducing what you learn in some shape or form, usually by condensing it. It engages your mind in a creative effort. The more creative, the more memorable. It's the best way to learn.

Below are some common ways in which students revise. Circle your favourite methods and mark whether you think these are active or passive. Answers are provided below.

Revision method	Active or passive?
Re-reading	
Copying out	
Putting your notes on computer	
Highlighting	
Writing index cards	
Annotating your texts	
Mindmapping	
Repeating out loud	
Doing past papers	

Re-reading: passive

By re-reading your notes you take information in, but you don't try and recall it, so you can't check how well you have absorbed the material – and the chances are that you won't absorb it very well because you are doing nothing to seal it in your mind.

Copying out: passive

You may favour this method to alleviate your sense of guilt that you're not working enough, while continuing to avoid work. Copying material out takes ages, but it doesn't engage your mind: you're working in a mechanical, secretarial fashion. While half your brain is absorbed with the writing task, there is only half left with which to take in the contents.

There's also a risk that copied-out notes look so neat and 'samey' that they fail to make as much impression on your memory as your old, scruffy notes in varying styles.

Putting your notes on computer: passive

Passive revision isn't taxing

Unless you have a specific need to have certain material on disk, isn't this a complete waste of time, for all the reasons outlined above, with the added temptation to spend hours messing about with layout and special fonts.

Highlighting: passive

Highlighting is a popular student activity because it requires no effort at all other than recognition – in other words, noticing important passages. If you highlight your notes, you probably have some reason to procrastinate in your work, as you put off learning your material and satisfy yourself instead with earmarking it. By making your notes fluorescent, you don't necessarily make them easier to learn – you just boost the profits of fluorescent pen manufacturers.

Writing index cards: active

By summarising material on index cards you attempt to say it all over again in fewer words. This method draws your attention to topics that you need to understand better. Summarising also goes some way towards learning, and makes material easy to refer back to.

The downside is that this method can be time-consuming and dull, as you will probably agree if you've ever devoted an evening to writing out index cards. Personally, I get more joy from mind-mapping (more about that later).

> **I need a systematic way of getting through all my revision.**
>
> This method is boring but simple. Divide up all your subjects into separate topics. Read through your topics to gain a sense of overview, then reduce their essentials onto a sheet or two of A4. Learn that.

Annotating your texts: active

By annotating the texts you read with your comments and summaries, you make an effort to digest their meaning. You have to work out what a passage is about, and say it in a nutshell. You also make your notes personal, and therefore more memorable, since they start to make sense to you in your own way. It's worth picking up a pencil every time you read, so that you get into the habit of making simultaneous notes.

Active revision involves reproducing ideas . . .

Notice how this book has been annotated for you:

① *By making notes*

- Paragraph contents are summarised in the margins using short phrases or keywords
- Section contents are summarised at the top of the right-hand page
- Chapter contents are summarised under chapter headings

This method is less intrusive than highlighting or underlining, because it fills margins but keeps text clean and uncluttered. That's a real advantage if you're making notes on creative writing which you may wish to read again without being distracted by your own additions.

Saves re-reading

Not only does note-taking of this kind help you memorise the relevant contents of your texts, as you will realise once you start thinking up your own annotations, rather than just reading mine. It saves you looking for needles in haystacks: key passages become extremely easy to track down. To facilitate this further, I normally include a keyword referring to important passages or quotations at the top of each relevant page. (I haven't done that in this book, but you can add these yourself if you like.)

This book has been annotated in fairly conservative fashion, due to the limitations imposed by print and by the need to make

Use shorthand
e.g.

important: |
confusing: ⟨
interesting: ⅋

Annotate
selectively

sense to a wide readership; however, you can make notes in any way you like, using your own brand of shorthand. If you have a visual imagination, a picture saves a thousand words: sketching what you see as you read will help to seal the information in your memory. Converting material into a quick table or chart often makes learning considerably easier. You can represent causes, consequences and other relationships between points using mathematical symbols such as arrows, percentage signs, equals signs and so on.

I use a straight vertical line to mark out important passages, a confusing wiggly vertical line to mark sections I don't really understand and may wish to return to later, exclamation marks or question marks for material that I find surprising or curious. I have a special symbol, that looks like a ribbon, for anything I find interesting if not useful.

I've annotated this entire book. It's very rare that you would do the same in your revision, since at higher levels, you would rarely read a book from cover to cover unless it's a set text. Therefore, it's only worth making notes on passages that are relevant to you.

Mindmapping: active

This is a very creative and personal way to digest your notes. I explain more about this technique in the following sections.

Repeating out loud: active

②
By talking

Talking
deepens
insights

Sing-songs aid
recall

Whether you get someone to test you, speak to the wall or into a cassette recorder, there's something magical about talking out loud that forces you to make creative links from one idea to the next. Teachers are very familiar with this process, finding they gain fresh insights into their subject simply by explaining it to others. And certainly, if you are a language student, aim as far as possible to speak your target language as you work.

If you're trying to learn a list of things, you could do worse than to chant it over and over again – for instance, if you were ever taught the various fates of the wives of Henry VIII, you probably repeated, 'Divorced, beheaded, died, divorced, beheaded, survived'. Better still if it rhymes: who can forget to remember, remember the fifth of November? It's by repetition, particularly sung repetition, that advertisers on TV and radio get us to learn their catchphrases. It's by repetition, particularly sung repetition, that advertisers . . . you get the point.

Doing past papers: active

③
By practising

This is the most active revision you can do in preparation for your exams, because doing past papers makes you recollect everything you have learnt that's relevant to the question and familiarises you with the format of your exams. This issue is discussed further in Chapter 5.

Map out your notes

And now, back to mindmapping. An excellent alternative to traditional note-taking, this is a really useful study technique, worth trying if you've never used it before. Because it makes use of colour, drawing and space, it's thought to stimulate the creative, right side of the brain, giving your cognitive processes an extra boost, and making light work of memorising what's on the page.

Mindmaps boost brainpower

Many students tell me they've tried mindmaps but that 'they don't really work'. In every case, I've found the person misuses the technique in some way or other; therefore, I still recommend that you read on.

To introduce you to mindmaps, I've drawn a few myself, as I'm sure you've noticed: they summarise chapter contents at the end of each chapter (apart from Chapter 6, which shows you a sample essay plan instead). These maps are quite basic – I didn't want to make them too daunting for you to look at (other people's mind maps often seem terrifyingly clever). Therefore, in drawing up your own mindmaps, you can go into many more layers of detail than I've done in this book. If you like, you can even use A3 paper to map out a large topic.

Use my mindmaps as basic templates

To make information even easier to record and recall, follow these additional guidelines:

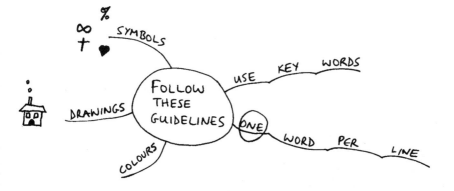

Uses of mindmaps

Mindmaps aid
revision . . .

Mindmaps are rather less suited to mathematical subjects and rather more appropriate for subjects like biology and all arts subjects involving essay writing. If you wish to include equations or quotations, I suggest you write these out in full in a corner underneath your map. You can refer to them in your map in keyword form.

+ essays

In fact, mindmaps aren't just useful for revision and note-taking: they make good preparation for written work. When I use mindmaps to plan my own essays (yes, I still write essays) I don't bother with colours. I number the branches and add a branch for the introduction and another for the conclusion. However, if the essay is complex, I still draw up a point-by-point plan after drawing up a mindmap. First, the map gives me inspiration and freedom in my thoughts. Then, the linear plan consolidates my structure.

Mindmap
practice

If you wish to try your hand at mindmapping, you need an easy topic to start you off. How about this one: '*The disadvantages of living in capital cities*'. Give yourself ten minutes to draw up your map. Do so freely and spontaneously, without worrying too much about where your ideas should go. Use a different colour for each new branch. You may find yourself hesitating about whether to extend an existing branch or create a new one. If in doubt, create a new branch: you can show an important link between ideas on separate branches with an arrow or colour coding.

Mindmap dos and don'ts

Have you done your map? Mine is on the next page. Look at it now but don't worry if yours isn't quite the same. The main thing is that you noticed the following advantages of mindmapping:

Mindmaps free
up thinking

- More speed in writing points down
- More flow in your ideas
- New ideas triggered more easily
- Easy organisation of material
- Easy insertion of new branches with every new idea

Look over your mindmap: if your thinking is confused, your map will reflect that.

First, check that you have used only *one word per branch*. If you wrote phrases, you will have blocked your ideas. For instance, the word 'pollution' on its own brings up associations like 'air', 'noise' or 'litter', and the word 'traffic' brings up 'congestion', 'pollution'

Disadvantages of living in capital cities

and 'travel'; but if you write 'capital cities have a pollution problem because there is a lot of traffic' you close off these associations – and waste time.

See illustration below

Second, look at the way you linked your branches. Each branch is like a main heading for the branch that follows it. Therefore, 'air', 'noise' and 'litter' all come off 'pollution', but they must be on separate branches, because they are different categories leading to different ideas. For instance, 'air' leads to the subcategory 'asthma', 'noise' to the subcategory 'stress' and 'litter' leads to the subcategory 'rats' – this in turn leads to the subcategory 'disease'. If you put 'pollution', 'air', 'noise' and 'litter' one after the other, you confuse categories and subcategories, and also limit the development of your ideas.

Check that you wrote *on the line*, and not in an empty space *next* to the line. Many people draw a line and then a gap, followed by another line with another gap: thus, on an unconscious level, they

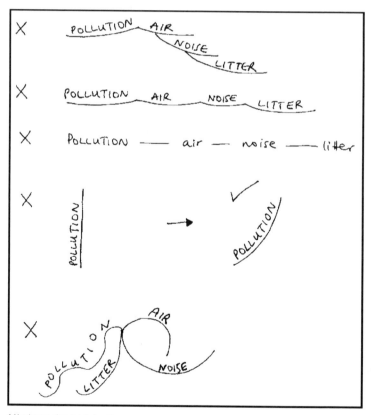

Mindmap dos and don'ts

interrupt the natural links in their train of thought. Let the branches connect directly with each other, and write neatly above them.

Finally, is your map easy to look over or do you have to crane your neck to read it? If so, where your branches point south, bend them a little east or west, so that you can still write above the line.

Ruler-straight lines indicate a rigid thinker, so practise being more flexible. You might try to be more spontaneous, or try to think more laterally, so that you start to see ideas from different points of view.

If, on the other hand your lines are overly wavy, you may lack structure and be too pliable: stick to the main arguments to develop more rigour in your work.

If you've tried these ideas and you like the technique, keep using it whenever you see fit. Mindmapping is best taught on a one-to-one basis: if you get stuck, you might be able to find someone who can use the technique and show you how to adapt it to your own *Horses for* work. If not, don't worry about it. Mindmaps don't suit everyone. *courses* People who are visually stimulated, who have a vivid imagination and enjoy doodling take better to mindmaps than others. You may prefer using index cards or taping your ideas: stick to your preferred method of working if it does the trick for you.

Memory tricks

Parts of your learning will lend themselves to being speeded up using various mnemonics. These are memory tricks which link up points and make them stand out, facilitating recall of key *Mnemonics* ideas and fiddly detail. They also make it easy to remember what *boost recall* order various sequences come in. Mnemonics make revision an altogether more enjoyable and confident process.

(but still Be warned: no system is magic. You still have to revise after a day, *require revision* a week, a month and a term; however, mnemonics make your *as on p. 86)* material quick to run through your mind and you'll find that after a few revisions you stop needing them as props – the material will stick in your mind.

Some easy mnemonics follow. Some are visual, others auditory. Pick whichever you like best.

Put elements together in one frame

Sketch all the elements you need to learn, so that they are connected in your picture. Let's say you wanted to remember two of

Martin Luther's important changes to religious practice. One change was to allow priests to marry. He also changed services from Latin to the common language. You could combine these elements in one frame, by drawing a wedding ceremony between a priest and his bride with speech bubbles in Latin crossed out and replaced by speech bubbles in English.

Combine points in a picture

That's a simple example. If you like this technique, you can use it to illustrate more complex combinations.

Make phrases from first letters

If you enjoy playing with words, you may find you can make up sentences or phrases that encapsulate the first letters of words in a list. For instance, can you remember the Seven Deadly Sins? Not quite? In sequence, these are:

Acronym-style mnemonics

Pride, **E**nvy, **A**nger, **S**loth, **C**ovetousness, **G**reed, **L**ust

You can remember them by memorising the following phrase:

Punishment **E**nsures **A**ll **S**erious **C**riminals **G**et **L**icked

The method has one serious limitation: it's time-consuming unless you can quickly work out a phrase that makes any sense (this one took me five minutes). However, once you've worked it out, remembering your sequence is no trouble at all.

> **I don't like using mnemonics involving word-play. Is there something wrong with me?**
>
> No. You may have a more visual imagination, as illustrated by the case of a 6-year-old who persistently spelt 'because' as 'becaftwo'. She had been taught the mnemonic 'big elephants can't always use small exits'. It worked for everyone else in the class, but she was a particularly imaginative child, rather more sensitive to the image of a trapped elephant and rather less attuned to the sounds of the alphabet, and so the phrase that stuck in her mind was: 'big elephants can't always find the way out'.

Scrabble words from first letters

This is exactly the same principle, but instead of sentences you create words, as you would do if you were playing Scrabble. For instance, a well-known sporting mnemonic is the word 'RICE': each letter represents a different stage in the procedure you should follow if you sprain yourself:

1 **R**est
2 **I**ce
3 **C**ompression
4 **E**levation

The bad news is that the success of this type of mnemonic rests entirely on what letters you have to hand. You need a good balance of vowels and consonants, and not too many awkward letters like X, J and Z – as you'll agree if you've ever played Scrabble. The good news is that now you know exactly what to do if you ever twist your ankle.

Create stories

String together items in a list, by making up a story that combines them. Here's how I remember the planets, starting with Pluto, which is furthest from the sun, and ending with Mercury, which is nearest and therefore hottest:

Pluto the Disney dog sang a **tune (Neptune)** about his favourite topic, his **urine (Uranus)**. He sang so poignantly that he was asked to sing in the local nightclub that **Saturday (Saturn)**. He was absolutely thrilled, accepted the offer, and, come Saturday, drove over to the nightclub in his **Jeep (Jupiter)**. Unfortunately, disaster struck. The Jeep ground to a halt: it was stuck on a **Mars Bar** that someone carelessly left on the ground. Oh no! Was he going to miss his special evening? A kindly **earthworm (Earth)** popped his head out of the ground. 'I'll help you,' he offered, 'I can eat my way through this chocolate bar, and free you.' **Venus**, the goddess of love, watching from the heavens, was mightily impressed by his generosity (a Mars Bar is quite a lot for such a tiny creature) and promptly fell in love with the worm. In the heat of her passion, her temperature rose: the **mercury** in her thermometer burst and she became as hot as the sun.

String chapter summaries together in a story

To remember entire paragraphs in sequence, go through your material, reducing it down to one keyword per paragraph. Make that keyword a concrete noun, so that you can easily picture it in your mind. It can be a word that already exists in the text, or any other word that you think effectively summarises the content.

For instance, let's imagine you had to learn the stress response outlined in Chapter 2. Here's the relevant information again, followed by my suggested keywords:

- Blood flow is instantly directed away from the skin, digestive tract, kidneys, liver and immune system, and delivered in extra quantities to brain, heart and muscles [**vital organs**].
- The heart beats faster, pumping more blood to muscles [**pump**].
- Blood pressure rises [**blood pressure**].
- Muscles tense up, ready for action [**muscles**].
- Breathing becomes fast and shallow, to increase oxygen intake [**oxygen**].
- Pupils dilate, taking in more light [**pupils**].
- The liver releases stored sugar – levels of sugar, fat and cholesterol rise in the bloodstream, providing extra energy [**sugar**].
- Levels of platelets and blood clotting agents increase in the blood, to protect from excess bleeding in case of injury [**platelets**].
- Perspiration increases [**sweat**].

Now string your keywords together in a story. Mine is from the Bible:

Put the words
in a silly story

The whale, having eaten Jonah, was making ready to digest his **vital organs**. However, being (in this version) a well-prepared diver, Jonah was ready to fight back with a **pump** he had brought along just in case this kind of thing happened. He pumped up the whale; the whale's **blood pressure** rose, as the air pressure builds up in a bicycle tyre. Irritated, it burped up Jonah (whales have strong burp **muscles**). Once released, Jonah took a gasp of nice, clean **oxygen**, and felt much better. Versatile Jonah was not only a diver, but also a teacher, and so he told his **pupils** all about this incident during school dinner . . . which in this curious educational establishment consisted of nothing but **sugar** piled up on little child-sized red **plates**. The story terrified these children, so that they all came out in a great cold **sweat**, and could not eat.

Use memory hooks

So far we've looked at ways of linking keywords directly together by putting them in stories. Sometimes that's easy. Sometimes, though, stories can grow unruly, in which case, it's simpler to hang keywords onto 'memory hooks'. Let me explain.

Say you have ten keywords to remember. For simplicity's sake, I've chosen the ten signs of the zodiac corresponding to the months from January to October, in sequence. Unless you're an astrology buff, you're likely to be as vaguely familiar with these as you are with aspects of your notes that you need to learn.

Alternatively,
hang keywords
on memory
hooks

All you need to do is to associate your keywords with the ten following easily remembered hook words:

gun, shoe, tree, door, hive, sticks, heaven, plate, wine, pen

'You must be joking! I can't remember all those words!' you gasp. Yes you can: they rhyme with the following unforgettable sequence: one, two, three, four, five, six, seven, eight, nine, ten! You can learn them right now and it will only take you a minute.

Learn the
zodiac

Once you've learnt your hook words, look at Table 4.1 to see how you can hang the zodiac words onto them. Now, don't cheat, and, without looking, recall which sign corresponds to number five.

'That's all very well,' you grumble, 'but there are twelve signs in the zodiac and so far we've only learnt ten, which leaves out Scorpio and Sagittarius. This system is no use beyond ten items.'

If you need more than ten hooks, you can make up your own, remembering to stick to concrete nouns, as these are easiest to picture in your mind. Let me start you off. Table 4.2 offers you a mix of rhyming, pictorial and symbolic hooks which should give you some ideas.

Table 4.1 How to use hook words to remember the zodiac

Hook word	Keyword	Association
1 gun	Capricorn	The goat is easily muddled with Aries. Therefore, I create a picture with a caper. Imagine wielding a fairground **gun**. To win a prize, shoot a tiny **caper** being blown about in the alcove facing you.
2 shoe	Aquarius	An **aquatic shoe** is a magic shoe that propels you when you swim (honest).
3 tree	Pisces	Imagine a **tree** bearing **fish** instead of fruit. If you don't easily associate Pisces with fish, imagine instead a tree bearing **pies**.
4 door	Aries	Imagine your front **door** made of **ram**'s wool. If you didn't know Aries was a ram, how would you like a front door made of **air**?
5 hive	Taurus	Imagine a cowardly Spanish **toreador** hiding in a **beehive**; or a **bull** that is particularly vengeful because it got **stung**.
6 sticks	Gemini	Imagine **twins** fighting with **sticks**. If you didn't know Gemini means twins, visualize walking-sticks encrusted with **gems**.
7 heaven	Cancer	The link between getting **cancer** and going to **heaven** is a strong one. If this is too painful, picture a **crab** dancing the cancan in **heaven**.
8 plate	Leo	Imagine a **lion** eating its kill on a fancy **dinner plate**.
9 wine	Virgo	Richard Branson's **wine** club, perhaps?
10 pen	Libra	Imagine a pair of **scales** balancing delicately on the end of a long **pen**.

Table 4.2 More hook words

Number	Hook	Explanation
11	Skis	Pictorial
12	Eggs	A dozen eggs
13	Horseshoe	For luck
14	Fort	Sounds like 'fourt(een)'

A set of picture hooks

Pictorial hooks

If you'd like another set of hooks with which to remember another list of ten items, see the picture hooks illustration overleaf for a picture sequence that's incredibly easy to recall.

Can I recycle hook systems without getting muddled between old and new associations?

Yes. If you learnt the zodiac, you can see this for yourself: write down ten household objects and memorise them with the same hook system. The zodiac won't interfere with your new associations.

If you want a mnemonic for *both* the zodiac list *and* the list of household items, it's best to use two different sets of hooks.

The good news is that these systems are like scaffolding: after a few repetitions, you don't need them any more and can recycle them for new lists.

Routine objects as hooks

In the rare event that you should need a sequence of hooks that goes on and on, here's one used by memory champions to memorise extraordinarily long lists.

Draw up a list featuring objects you come across in your daily routine, from the minute you wake up. The sequence might start as follows:

'Daily routine' hooks

My **alarm clock** wakes me up. I stare at the **ceiling**, then get up and look out of the **window** to see what the weather is like. I take off my **pyjamas** and I have a hot **shower**. Then it's off to the **kitchen** to eat breakfast: **toast** and **marmite** . . .

Your hooks are:

1	Alarm clock	5	Shower
2	Ceiling	6	Kitchen
3	Window	7	Toast
4	Pyjamas	8	Marmite . . . and so on

You can go on all day.

		Looks like...
1		Chewing gum
2		Hosepipe
3		Lightning
4		Satan
5		Clown
6		Cherry
7		Knee
8		Race track
9		Leaf
10		Coconut

Picture hooks

Remember numbers

Because they are symbols for abstract concepts, numbers are really not easy to remember *per se*. Many people unwittingly remember telephone numbers using a motor mnemonic: when they have a telephone keypad in front of them, their hand automatically moves to the right places. In other words, the movement of their hand is more memorable than the sequence of numbers.

Since telephone keypads aren't normally provided in exams, it's a good idea to use a mnemonic that can act, at the very least, as a backup for any number sequence you need to remember. The following explanations show how to learn historical dates, as this is a popular student request; but you can use the systems to help you learn anything involving sequences of numbers.

Numbers are hard to remember . . .

Numbers with special connotations

Some numbers are easy to remember because they have special connotations. Table 4.3 shows a few famous examples.

Table 4.3 Number associations

Number	Association
13	Unlucky
17	Driving test
21	Coming of age
69	(I daren't explain)
101	Room 101 from George Orwell's Nineteen Eighty Four; or 101 Dalmatians

I'm sure you remember many numbers of your own: a best year, a worst age, a house or bus number, various telephone numbers, and so on. Look out for dates and figures that you have to learn which contain these memorable numbers. Associate them as vividly as you can. For instance, the Russian revolution was in 1917. You know, I hope, that this happened last century. To remember the year, imagine the tsar being overthrown by a pack of Russian adolescents who had just passed their driving test, and drove all over him.

. . . but easy with tricks . . .

① *A 'simple 'familiar associations' mnemonic*

Associate numbers with consonants

This mnemonic system is more advanced, but it's well worth the effort if you want to be sure of your figures. It involves associating the numbers from 0 to 9 with a series of consonant sounds. Let's start by learning the sequence of sounds thrown up by the numbers 0 to 5, which you can do quickly and easily, using the prompts shown in Table 4.4. Take a few minutes now to study this.

Table 4.4 Numbers and consonants

Number	Consonant sounds	Prompt
0	s, z	Imagine a snake, curled up in a **0**-shaped ball, hissing: '**sss**'. **Z** is a similar sound.
1	t, d	Exaggerate in your mind's eye the **downstroke** of **t** and **d**.
2	n	**n** has **two** feet.
3	m	**m** has **three** feet.
4	r	Think of roar, which rhymes with **four**; or visualise a huge **r** at the end of the word fou**r**.
5	l	Think of the drink '**five** alive'; or think of the roman numeral **l** which stands for **50**.

You can already learn the date of Stalin's death: 1953. I'm sure you already know this was a twentieth-century event. All you need to remember is 53:

$$53 = l + m$$

One word you can make by adding vowel sounds is **lime**. Viable words are those for which, despite spelling, consonant sounds remain l and **m**. Other possibilities are **lamb** and **limb** (but not lamp or limp, because the 'p' is pronounced). For me, the most striking idea is the incongruous image of Stalin becoming meek as a lamb on his deathbed. Fix this picture in your mind in whatever way you like: draw it, if that helps you to visualise it. The idea is to associate Stalin's death with a lamb so that when you ask yourself, 'What year did Stalin die?' the picture of a lamb comes up, and you can work your way back to 53.

If you like this technique, I suggest you learn the rest of the sequence, from 6 to 9, as shown in Table 4.5. Revise the whole sequence for five minutes. (It might take you a few revisions to learn it very well.)

Table 4.5 More consonant prompts

Number	Consonant sounds	Prompt
6	ch, j, sh	**6** looks like a **ch**erry, if you colour it red; **j** and **sh** are very similar sounds.
7	k, hard g	Draw a horizontal mirror line through **K** and you get two **7**s lying back to back. As for hard **g**, you can remember that as a very similar sound to **k**.
8	f, v, th	**8** looks like an exaggerated loopy **f**; **v** and **th** are very similar sounds.
9	b, p	**P** is a mirror image of **9**. Flip it over and you get **b**, which is a very similar sound in any case.

Now you're ready for a couple of dates.

1 The first English dictionary was completed by Samuel Johnson in **1755**.
   17 = t/d + k/g = **dog**
   55 = l + l = **lily**
   Visualise a **dog** sitting proudly on the dictionary, holding a beautiful **lily** in its mouth.
2 Napoleon admitted defeat in the Battle of Waterloo by, shall we say, releasing a **dove** with a long **tail**. Can you work it out?

   Answer: 1815
   Tail = t + l = 15
   Dove = d + v = 18

Fix your centuries

Centuries can fall into place

If you like the system so far, you might find it useful to learn centuries in such a way that all the dates belonging to one century share one common element in the stories you make up. I've already suggested that the 1700s can be represented by 'dog', and the 1800s by 'dove'. A few more centuries are shown in Table 4.6.

This system has the advantage that you will never get your centuries mixed up again: a story you create with a tiara in it relates to a date in the 1400s; a hotel means a date in the 1500s, and so on. I know that the French Revolution, the American Declaration of Independence and the first English dictionary are all events belonging to the 1700s because in my stories they all involve dogs.

Table 4.6 How to remember centuries using words

Century	Letters	Word
1400	t/d + r	tiara
1500	t/d + l	hotel
1600	t/d + ch/sh/j	tissue
1700	t/d + k/g	dog
1800	t/d + f/v	dove

This is a challenge for your imagination; it will develop and blossom. Soon, you'll become an expert at the bizarre and eccentric . . . which is probably not a bad thing.

I like the system but sometimes I muddle letters. Is that not a bit risky?

The more you use the system, the less you will need it – numbers and dates will become firmly ingrained in your mind.

However, when using the mnemonic in an exam, I recommend you quickly write it out to check that you relate letters back to the correct numbers.

In a nutshell

There's plenty you can do to make your memory an extremely reliable tool. As well as making your learning active, you can ensure perfect recall by revising at four optimum points; after:

(A day)　(A week)　(A month)　(A term)

In addition, you can use mnemonics with which to seal strings of keywords, facts and dates in your mind. These all work on the same principle, that by condensing information and converting it into pictures, sounds and stories, it becomes instantly memorable.

Broadly speaking, by learning in this way you stimulate the brain's right hemisphere, which enjoys having a bit of fun but is left totally cold by logic. Therefore, feel free to make up colourful associations that make no sense at all. The crazier, more vulgar, more dramatic and exaggerated the idea, the better you will remember it.

Run these crazy stories through your mind again and again, just as you would revise anything. Soon, you will stop needing them as the material will stick in your mind anyway.

I guarantee that if you follow these guidelines in your exam preparation, your facts and figures will flow abundantly, like wine from a Roman fountain. Now there's a poetic image for you to take into your exams!

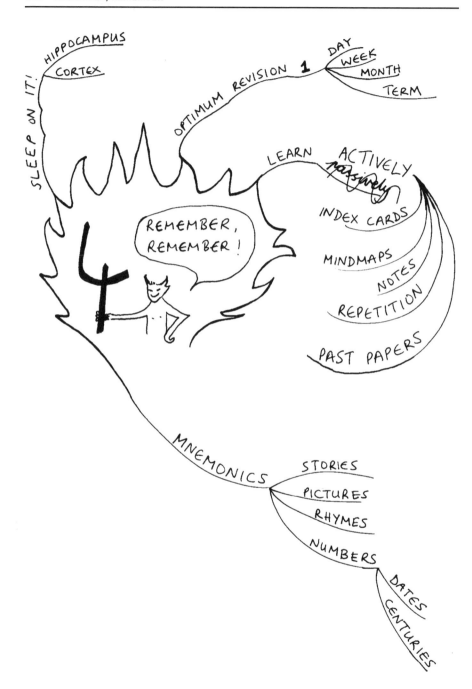

5

Use resources wisely

- Learning from examiners' feedback
- Coursework and revision priorities
- Good use of books, tutorials and lectures
- Internet tips

Imagination is more important than knowledge.

Albert Einstein

Develop a revision strategy . . .

Now that you know how to study effectively and master your memory, you're probably champing at the bit to do some serious learning. Steady on. Before you go off and learn volumes of irrelevant data, let's make sure you have an intelligent strategy that helps you develop proper exam skills. You want to make the most of your resources – your books, tutors, the Internet and so on. Time, of course, is perhaps the most precious resource of all. Here's how you can use it wisely.

Clarify your goals

Examiners tend to report the same failings in students' work. This is because students tend not to organise their revision along the right lines, as you can see for yourself:

Examiners' most common complaints and their most common causes

1 Complaint   Doesn't answer the question: contains irrelevant material.
Cause   *Doesn't know how to interpret question correctly and plan relevant answer.*

. . . based on examiners' feedback

2 Complaint   Too vague: doesn't define anything in the question that needs clarification. Issues are interpreted very loosely and so the work doesn't mean anything precise.
Cause   *Doesn't understand where clarification and specifics are needed; shallow planning.*

3 Complaint   Contradicts instructions in various ways, for instance by showing only one side of an issue that was meant to be discussed; answering the wrong number of questions; missing out parts of questions; expanding where was instructed to be brief, and being brief where instructed to expand.
Cause   *Doesn't understand exam instructions; no checking procedure.*

4 Complaint   Explains too little: gives facts, but doesn't make sense of them; shows figures without putting them in context; quotes, but doesn't explain what quotations express.
Cause   *Revision over-emphasised accumulation of knowledge without practising planning and developing ideas.*

5 Complaint   Too subjective: personal anecdotes and rhetorical statements outstrip academic evidence.
Cause   *Hasn't read enough essays to grasp academic register.*

6 Complaint   Doesn't use specialist terms and ignores those in the question.
Cause   *Revision didn't include learning specialist vocabulary and definitions.*

7 Complaint   Illegible; pages not clearly marked; questions not numbered.
Cause   *Underestimates value of practical details in exams: revision didn't include practising writing legibly under pressure.*

8 Complaint Silly mistakes with facts and figures.
Cause *Revision didn't include checking work accurately.*

9 Complaint Poor syntax: long, tedious or ungrammatical sentences.
Cause *Revision didn't include writing lucidly under time pressure.*

10 Complaint Rushed endings.
Cause *Revision didn't include timekeeping.*

Strategy first, knowledge acquisition last

The reason why students make these mistakes isn't necessarily that they don't know their subject. More often than not, they have the required knowledge – more than enough, in fact. They just haven't practised regurgitating it in the right format.

①
*Consider
what's required
of you . . .*

*. . . before you
start learning*

Many students prepare for coursework and exams by learning *first*, and finding out *last* what exam and coursework requirements they must meet. In other words, they go to lectures and take copious notes (or feel that they ought to). They read books from cover to cover (or feel that they ought to). Then and only then do they read their syllabus properly, look at past papers and, if they have time and inclination, practise exam-style questions.

It's the wrong way round.

I did very badly in a recent exam. Now I'm worried about all exams.

Did you realise there was a problem while you were in the exam? If so, your exam preparation was poor: you probably did too much background reading and not enough timed exam-style questions, or you may have missed out parts of your syllabus.

If your poor result came as a complete shock, the greatest likelihood is that you misinterpreted questions, in which case you need more planning practice (see Chapter 6).

Your top four study guides

1 Syllabus

This is your first priority as it tells you what you're aiming for. Your syllabus can guide you in your coursework, outlining which areas you must cover. It also tells you what topics you must include in your revision, or whether you can choose from a selection of topics. Where you do have a choice, it's safe policy to revise twice as many topics as you need to answer in the exam (unless you are confident that you can answer any question on your speciality). If in doubt, ask a tutor.

Syllabuses offer scope for originality

In arts subjects, it might pay to prepare some less popular options, where your work stands a better chance of originality. For instance, in an English syllabus, Shakespeare and Milton will be popular choices. You may make an impression by directing your interests towards lesser-known authors and revising the more unusual themes on your syllabus (Shakespeare's songs, for instance). It can be very rewarding to wander off the beaten track and do something imaginative.

2 Mark schemes and examiners' reports

Mark schemes are used by examiners to award or deduct points. They show what percentage of marks can (or can't) be gained by good structure, illustration, graphics, presentation, grammar, spelling, etc. Examiners' reports comment on the quality of previous years' coursework and exam papers. They explain what examiners do and don't like, and point out classic mistakes that students make in the subject.

Mark schemes + reports give dos + don'ts

Either of these are gold dust.

3 Model answers

These may be helpful, particularly in coursework where you can learn by example how to do a good essay. Coursework that scored well in previous years may inspire you. You may find model answers useful in preparing a science exam. However, they're not so useful in arts subjects, where answers are less black and white.

Model answers: Sciences ✓ Arts ✗

4 Past papers

These are a must, even in the initial stages of your revision, in order to become acquainted with the format of your exams and to practise applying your existing knowledge to exam questions. Look

Past papers ✓ ✓ ✓

over a few years' worth to assess what range of topics you need to revise, and to what depth.

In the final stages of your revision, aim to do plenty of practice based on sample questions. Follow the planning guidelines in the next chapter and find a tutor who is willing to mark your efforts.

Note that if your syllabus has changed in the last year, you should be given pilot papers, so you know what to expect. In addition to these, you can still work selectively from previous years' papers.

Face those past papers

Past papers stretch you

Although doing practice papers is one of the most useful ways you can prepare for your written exams, you may find yourself avoiding this task and feel compelled to do more research first. Research can be a way of putting off writing, because it's a relatively straightforward activity. Doing past papers requires considerable self-discipline: not only is it an effort, but it also threatens to expose your ignorance.

However, fear of ignorance isn't a good enough reason to avoid doing past papers. What's more, you fool yourself if you think time spent doing further reading is necessarily time spent constructively. Knowledge isn't everything: technique matters just as much, as it enables you to *use* what you know. Therefore, practise working under timed conditions so that you become proficient at dividing up your tasks, organising your time, developing your ideas while sticking to the point, recalling useful facts and figures, and so on. (The next chapter offers help on essay technique if you need it.)

Understand instructions

Instructions need preparation

Table 5.1 shows some typical exam instructions, demystified. Don't learn them all, but do prepare for those that may come up in your exams.

As you look over past papers, read the exam instructions and make sure you know *precisely* what they mean. Instructions make a huge difference to how you organise your answer. For instance, if you are instructed to *compare*, you must find similarities *and* differences; whereas if you are asked to *contrast*, you should find differences but *not* find similarities.

Table 5.1 Exam instructions, demystified

Instruction	Meaning
Account/give an account of	Give reasons for
Analyse	Give a detailed description, separating into different parts; investigate
Assess	Show how important or successful
Calculate	Find the value of and show your working
Comment	Give your opinion
Compare	Find similarities and differences, then weigh up whether the items have more or less in common
Consider	Think about; explain
Contrast/ distinguish between/ differentiate	Find differences
Define	Give exact meaning of
Demonstrate	Show how, using examples
Describe	Give a detailed account of
Discuss	Examine important aspects of; argue all sides before drawing a conclusion one way; outline the arguments, backing them up with evidence; consider the implications
Evaluate	Weigh up the value of a theory or idea in the light of evidence, giving your opinion
Examine	Look closely into
Explain	Paraphrase; give reasons for; interpret
Explore	Examine from every viewpoint
How . . .	In what way. Such questions are answered with 'by', not 'because'
Illustrate	Show by giving examples, diagrams or drawings
Interpret	Give the meaning of
Justify	Give evidence for a particular point of view, anticipating counterarguments
Outline	Describe without detail; give main features. Do this showing how points connect, develop or relate to other points
State	Present clearly but briefly
Summarise	Give the main points, without detail or examples
Trace	Show how a topic has developed from beginning to end

Exploit your sources of information

Now that you've got your priorities straight, you can turn your attention to the information sources which will help you organise your revision.

②
Start learning

Get the most out of your tutors

Tutor skills

Self-sufficiency

Assertiveness

Discuss goals

Your tutor is there to help you. At least, that's the theory. Just don't expect the same support you might have had from schoolteachers. This is partly because at higher levels you're expected to be self-sufficient. Moreover, some academics are more interested in research than in teaching. Many also resist putting great effort into tutorials. This is often because tutors commonly complain that once students get beyond UCAS, they lose interest in their subjects.

This suggests that you should be explicit with your tutor about what you want from the course, and what you think you need to consolidate. Today's fee-paying students are more assertive than students of my generation. I now wish I had dared to spell out what I found helpful and what I didn't, as this would have enabled me to learn more from certain tutors who, though academically brilliant, were disorganised and had a tendency to digress.

If you have certain ambitions that you would like to fulfil on your course, tell your tutor what your goals are. Many excellent students have no idea how capable they are, and assume mediocrity – a frank discussion with a helpful tutor could enlighten you.

Although a tutor should never be insulting about you or your work, tutoring means criticising, pushing and prodding. Some tutors evade this rather unpleasant business by stroking your ego and turning the whole tutorial into a cosy tea-and-muffins affair. Insist on being given directions as to how to improve your work.

I don't know how to cope with my tutor: I find her impossible to please.

You may be luckier than you think. A demanding tutor is often one who forces you to break new ground.

Try to switch your focus away from pleasing your tutor and towards finding a higher purpose in your learning. The most rewarding work is that which you do for yourself – not anyone else.

Constructive critism

Other tutors may be critical but not constructive. Distinguish between tutors who offer you an opportunity to improve your work and those who simply discourage you. If you only vaguely understand what you did wrong, ask for precise details. Don't let a paid professional get away with lazy marking like 'Lacks a sustained argument', 'Quite good' or 'Deficient in certain areas'. You have a right to know what the argument ought to be or where the deficiencies lie.

To ask this, you need courage, especially as tutors often underestimate how stinging some of their comments can be. Students show me essays covered in red ink, negative comments eclipsing the positive aspects of their work, their tutors' disparaging words still ringing in their ears. Remember that *you are not your work*. If you didn't make mistakes, there would be no need for you to have an education in the first place.

Destructive criticism

Another common problem is that tutors misjudge omissions on students' part as laziness. If you did put in the work, and your tutors accuse you of complacency, don't sit there aghast. Explain your side and you may find that your tutor becomes more helpful. It's often useful to ask your tutor to advise you on priority reading material. Tutors don't always know what's on your reading list; tell them and they may suggest better ideas. At higher levels, it's acceptable to request guidance on texts, because there are so many to choose from.

Misunderstandings

In a tutorial, you may wish to avoid repeating, 'I didn't catch what you said; could you say that again?' (although it's perfectly legitimate for you to ask this). Rather than nod blankly, repeat what you *think* you heard. This technique normally prompts the speaker to tell the listener more on the subject. Another way to pin tutors down is by email. They can write back in their own time – this may encourage them to look something up for you – and you can re-read their advice. For booklists, this is particularly helpful because it saves you the tedium and embarrassment of asking tutors to spell out authors' names.

Ask for clarification

There's nothing like having something in writing. The comments and references your tutors write on your essays may turn out to be incredibly helpful in your revision – more helpful than anything else, since these will point out areas that you need to consolidate, or aspects worth expanding. Therefore, don't hesitate to make notes of gems that arise in your tutorials (or immediately after), and leave ample space in your assignments to encourage your tutor to decorate your work with pearls of wisdom. I even suggest that you let the last line of your essays overflow onto a lovely, new, clean page. That's an invitation few tutors turn down.

Preserve tutors' comments

Get more out of your lectures

Lecture problems: too general/ specialised

Lectures and seminars aren't always directly helpful: they tend to be course-directed in science subjects, but in other subjects can cover specific topics of interest to the lecturer, disregarding the syllabus. At other times, they may be too general. This isn't to say that you shouldn't go: you may gain great insights from a good lecturer, whatever the topic. You may even wish to specialise in some of these areas at a later date.

Why did I keep daydreaming in lectures?

When you daydream, you take a sneaky break. It's possible that you worry about information overload, an anxiety that often starts at school and makes people switch off.

It's easily done because you can think at a much greater speed than a teacher or lecturer can talk. Humans can process up to 800 words per minute but can only speak at about 200. This disparity offers many daydreaming opportunities. Taking selective notes is one way to keep your mind on the lecture.

Prepare background

To get the most from your lectures, it helps, if you have time, to prepare a bit for those whose titles you know in advance, so that you have some notion of the books or topics they cover. This doesn't mean that you should swot! Just look over key works, so that you don't get caught out completely cold.

Take discriminating notes

It takes some skill to strike a balance between taking too many notes and failing to keep up with the lecturer, and taking too few notes and having nothing to refer back to. You certainly need to write phrases rather than single words: single words rarely make sense when you read them back. However, you haven't got time to write everything down, so try to discriminate. Think primarily of your revision aims. A good lecturer should introduce the structure and purpose of his or her talk: this can help you figure out what to look out for. It also shows you by example how a piece of academic reasoning can be put together, which is useful for the wording and structure of your own coursework and exam preparation.

By avoiding taking irrelevant notes, you retain your critical faculties because you don't allow yourself to sink into passive mode. If I insist on this point, it's simply because I took copious notes at university lectures, and realised before my exams that most were of no relevance at all – they ended up in the bin.

Here are other suggestions to keep you on your toes:

- Jot down exam-style questions that could be derived from the lecture content. You can reserve the margin of your page for these questions and for other questions or comments that come to mind during the lecture. This makes it easy to review.
- Second-guess what the lecturer is about to say. See if you can sketch an outline of his or her talk, on paper or in your head, so that you develop a sense of structure.

Probe and question

- Use question and answer sessions in seminars to flex your mind, even if you don't ask anything yourself. Simply place yourself in the lecturer's shoes whenever someone else asks a question and try to guess what the response might be. If there's something you haven't understood, ask!
- After the lecture, try to recall those elements that could feature in an exam question. You can make linear notes or sketch out a mindmap (for mindmapping help, see Chapter 4). Use arrows, pictures or diagrams that come to mind. Now that you have a better sense of the whole, think further on the issues: do you agree with the lecturer's views? If so, could they be expanded to other topics? If not, what's your own opinion? Jot down your own arguments, so that you develop your own thinking skills rather than just trying to reflect someone else's.

Revise lectures

I recommend you glance over your notes just before the next lecture. If you keep the same notepad that's easy enough. These revisions only take a few seconds, yet quickly amount to a remarkable knowledge base.

I'd like to contribute more to tutorials, lectures and seminars but I'm scared of asking stupid questions or making obvious points.

Everyone I know shares the same fear.

Ask away. The chances are, others won't have understood either, so they'll all be secretly grateful to you for daring to clarify the issue.

As for stating your views, have you considered the possibility that someone in the group could be inspired by what you say?

Exploit your friends and enemies

Whether you like them or not, your peers are a wonderful resource. They're on the same course as you, maybe a year ahead – perfect.

Talk to peers

Listen to what they have to say about coursework and exams. If they're good, read their essays. Their tutors might have told them something yours haven't. They may have a reference that you didn't know about, one that sorts out all your problems. Usually, the most helpful conversations happen at the most impromptu moments – a quick gossip outside a lecture hall can bring academic enlightenment.

Some students meet up regularly to help each other with their work and share resources. For instance, the cost of subscriptions to academic websites can be affordable if split among a group. You can get considerable support from revision groups, particularly when they're well organised and the people in them share a common purpose.

Research effectively

Higher level reading = needles in haystacks

At higher levels of education, you need to develop autonomy in your research. Tutorials and lectures can't cover the syllabus in sufficient depth. Because the research you do is likely to be undirected, try to work out a game plan before you start.

Use books selfishly

At school, your textbooks were specially devised to follow the course curriculum. This isn't like school: for goodness sake, don't read source material from cover to cover, as it's highly unlikely to match your exact requirements. You will have enormous booklists to wade through, but very few listed titles will contain much more than a chapter's worth that's relevant to you.

When you read a book to gain information for your coursework or exam preparation, think as specifically as you can about what you're looking for. Here's a procedure to help you get to the jugular without wasting time:

1 Decide what information gaps you need to fill and set yourself a time limit.

Read from the end!

2 Start with the index and contents pages.

3 Look for possible chapter summaries. The last chapter may summarise the book.

Overview contents

4 Browse through a book as if you were in a bookshop, to glean information from the most relevant chapters.

5 Skim read, by glancing at headings and the first lines of paragraphs, until you find what you want.

Then select in-depth reading

6 Use the note-taking technique explained in Chapter 4 (see page 89). If you can't mark your texts, look away and write what you recall in your own shorthand, using keywords and phrases rather than full sentences. Alternatively, you could sketch a mindmap.

When you copy extracts from your sources that you wish to quote in your coursework, note the page number and mark the extract in inverted commas so that you distinguish it from your own notes. This will help you avoid plagiarising by mistake (more about plagiarism later). It's also worth noting the following references:

Make helpful notes (e.g. sources)

- Author's initial and surname. If there is no author, write the editor's name in brackets: (ed.)
- Date of publication
- Book title and subtitle
- Publisher
- Publisher's town

This saves you the tedium of having to seek out these references when you compile your bibliography. (You can use the bibliography at the back of this book as a template for your own.)

Speed-read

The speed with which you read depends on your purpose. In literature or poetry, you will come across passages that need to be read slowly, in meditative fashion. If you are reading through your notes, it makes sense to skip as you read. If you are a science student and have to digest complex equations, you need to do some persistent re-reading, until the information is fully absorbed.

Fast reading aids comprehension

Background reading needs to be done at a good pace. Most people read too slowly, under the common illusion that if they speeded up they would lose understanding. In fact, the reason why it's easy to lose concentration as you read is that your eyes can't read as they move: they have to keep stopping and starting, making hundreds of minute adjustments as they leap from word to word (slow readers) or from phrase to phrase (faster readers). By increasing your speed, you automatically push yourself to take in more words at a glance. This helps you to avoid distraction, gather momentum and gain a sense of overview which greatly facilitates comprehension.

To read fast, you must help your eyes by using a guide – a pencil will do, or your finger – and move the guide steadily across

Speed-reading
tips

the page. Try this now, as you read these lines. Choose a steady pace, one that's comfortable but pushes you just a tiny bit, so that you have to concentrate. It's the constancy of speed, rather than the speed itself, that saves you time, because it eliminates hesitations. If you come to a passage you don't understand, keep going. It will probably make sense with hindsight. If not, you can always go back to unravel it later, if it's relevant enough to bother.

Do this every day and you will quickly improve. Once you're reading quite fast, you can do what speed-readers do and cover the preceding line of text with a piece of paper. Push the paper down at a steady rate to cover lines as you read. (If you put the paper below your line of text, you risk slowing down your reading.)

To save yourself having to read anything twice, mark or annotate relevant passages as you go along. Chapter 4 explains how (see pages 88–90).

It's so unfair that there was no Internet in my day

You don't know your luck. You can press a few keys and get information from across the world on academic subjects (www. academicinfo.net), access reference books (www.britannica.com)

Background reading needs to be done at a good pace

and even get dodgy simultaneous translations (www.babelfish. altavista.digital.com). I had to cycle in the wind and the rain to distant libraries . . . only to be told that my book was out, or being mended, or lost.

Internet search
skills

I'm probably preaching to the converted here, but bear in mind that there's an art to using the Internet without getting sidetracked. Have your goals clearly in mind, and set a time limit before you start. The secret of success on the Internet is to be adept at searching. When you type in a search, use the following techniques:

- Inverted commas around a phrase request an exact match, as for 'President Roosevelt' (you aren't interested in other presidents, or in other Roosevelts).
- Uppercase requests uppercase. Use lowercase where you don't wish to discriminate between either upper or lower.
- Attach + to a word that you wish to be found in your search (e.g. Labour+party).
- Attach – to a word that you want excluded from your search (e.g. python–monty).
- An asterisk asks for wild cards, or variations (e.g. psycho* will bring up psychotherapy, psychology, psychopath . . .).

Look out also for 'advanced search' directions if you wish to narrow down your search even further. If you're having problems with your search word or phrase, try a little lateral thinking – a thesaurus (or thesaurus.com) might help you think up associated vocabulary.

How can I improve my chances of a successful search?
Use a variety of .com (or .co.uk) search engines such as Google, Altavista, Ask, Dogpile, Excite, Lycos, Search, Snap and Yahoo. This is because no single engine covers more than about 15 per cent of the worldwide web. Web Ferret (www.ferretsoft.com) searches the search engines for what you want.

Useful sites

There are hundreds of free sites you can access to help you research your subject on the Internet. Your own university website may give you useful links. Here are a few other suggestions:

- www.hw.ac.uk/libWWW/irn/pinakes/pinakes.html   Provided by Heriot-Watt University in Scotland, this site offers links to 32 excellent academic sites.

- www.studentzone.org.uk A student portal to academic sites, library sites (including the British Library) and resources for open and distance learning.
- www.odci.gov/cia/publications/factbook This is the CIA's World Fact Book: it contains a host of up-to-date maps, facts and figures and other data useful for students of geography, history and politics.
- www.infoplease.com This general knowledge network offers a dictionary, thesaurus and basic information on a variety of subjects such as history, geography, government, biography, business, society, culture, health, science and social science.
- www.ngfl.gov.uk The National Grid for Learning was set up by the UK government to improve standards in education at all levels. Type in your search, and gain access to other educational sites.
- www.nybooks.com/nyrev You can search this *New York Review of Books* site for current debate on a wide range of published issues.
- www.exosci.com Exoscience publishes regular scientific bulletins.
- www.newspapers.com This is the archive to the world's news-papers. (Alternatively, you can access individual newspapers' sites.)
- www.wikipedia.org A multilingual online encyclopaedia, famous for the fact that anyone can edit it, thereby supposedly making it particularly accurate and up to date.
- www.elibrary.com and www.search.eb.com (the *Encyclopaedia Britannica* Internet guide) enable you to download articles, essays and dissertations, which may (or may not) save you time and give you inspiration. However, these sites are not cheap, and not all the essays are of a high standard.

If a site offers many links that catch your eye, read through the list first, then bookmark your selection to avoid hopping from site to site.

www.time-saving tips

Where you have considerable material to plough through, I recommend printing it out rather than trying to read from the screen (it's also easier on your eyesight). To save yourself logging on and off as you print, copy and paste text from the Internet into an empty file, from which it's easier to print everything in one go, if necessary. If you only make occasional use of the Internet, one file suffices: mine is called 'bits & pieces' and I copy into it from the top down, so that newly added material appears first. If you make frequent use of the Internet, I recommend creating a special

Internet folder with subject files. Keeping everything in one place saves searching for it later.

The Internet's greatest asset is also its main limitation: size. You can waste hours and hours (and days and days) searching the web. For greater depth or for a better overview of your topic, you may actually save time and effort by braving the wind and the rain and asking a librarian. The modern librarian will invariably have undergone extensive training in using the Internet to source information.

The Internet can waste your time

In a nutshell

Contrary to popular belief, good coursework or exam preparation doesn't involve learning more and more about your subject: it means using your imagination and initiative to make profitable use of what you already know. You need to find out the variety of skills that your examiners want from you and then set about developing them, with the help of the information resources available to you.

If you can do this, you will succeed – not only in your current aim to pass your exams, but also in whatever task you take on in the future.

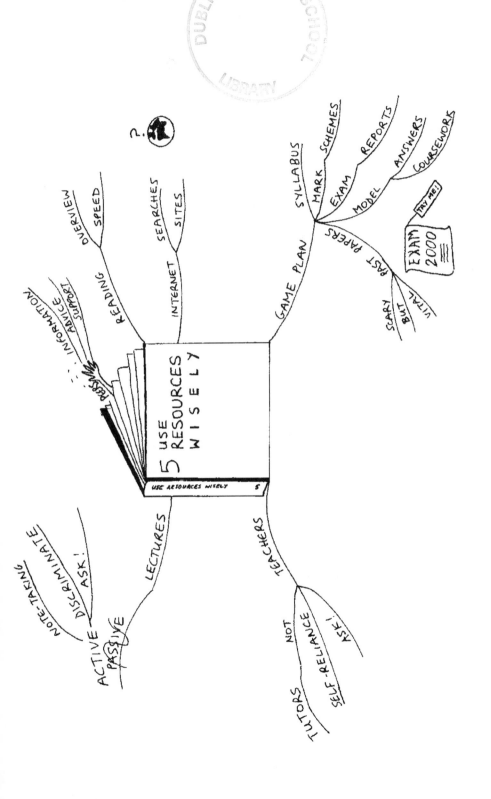

5 USE RESOURCES WISELY

USE RESOURCES WISELY   5

READING
— OVERVIEW
— SPEED

INTERNET
— SEARCHES
— SITES

BOOKS
— INFORMATION
— ADVICE
— SUPPORT

LECTURES
— ACTIVE
— PASSIVE
— NOTE-TAKING
— DISCRIMINATE
— ASK!

TEACHERS
— TUTORS
— NOT SELF-RELIANCE
— ASK!

GAME PLAN
— SYLLABUS
— MARK SCHEMES
— EXAM REPORTS
— MODEL ANSWERS
— COURSEWORK
— PAST PAPERS
— SCARY BUT VITAL

EXAM 2000
TRY ME!

?.

6

Plan for success

'And all your notes,' said Dorothea . . . 'All those rows of volumes – will you not make up your mind what part of them you will use, and begin to write the book which will make your vast knowledge useful to the world?'

George Eliot, *Middlemarch*

If you've read Chapter 5, you must realise by now that the success of your exams rests rather less on how much you know, and rather more on what you can do with what you know.

There will always be a voice inside your head nagging you to spend more time reading in libraries because you feel you ought to *Planning =* accumulate more wisdom. It's precisely because at higher levels *making use of* of education you can never know enough, that knowledge alone *knowledge* doesn't necessarily pay dividends. Rather than accumulating piles of notes (or feeling that you ought to), learn to do something useful with the ideas you already have. In other words, learn to plan.

Planning is really very important

If the thought of planning makes you groan, look back at the examiners' comments in Chapter 5 (see page 110): they show how few students plan their work properly.

The main reason why so many students resist planning is that it's about plunging in at the deep end: planning means *thinking*. That's quite an effort, and may lead to some difficult realisations, such as the fact that you probably have to fill in gaps in your knowledge, that your best ideas turn out to be irrelevant to the question, or that your points don't always fit very well together.

Therefore, you too may be tempted to hang it all and just start writing, in the vain hope that everything will work out in the end. Yet, a plan saves having to redraft (at higher levels, you don't have time for roughs). It also saves you giving your audience all the wrong messages – messages like:

- I don't really care.
- I'm going to say everything I know about this topic, never mind the question.
- You're the expert, so you pick out the relevant bits, if you can find them.
- I digress – I don't really understand the question . . . what was it again?
- I won't use paragraphs because I haven't considered what groups or categories my ideas fall into. In fact I might make my whole essay one lovely, long paragraph.
- I'll leave out the main points, or make them brief and under-developed, whereas my most banal points (and there will be lots) will occupy pages on end.
- I might change my mind halfway through and make my piece about something else that's a bit easier.
- Let me contradict myself: I'm working it out as I go along, OK?!
- I will never address the issue. But I will make it look like I'm about to.
- I shall stop abruptly when I dry up.
- I won't give you an overview of the subject.
- I shall draw conclusions that I can't justify.
- Quotes? Dates? Backup information? Ooops!

I hope this satisfies you that planning is always worthwhile, *especially* if you're pushed for time.

All right, I'll plan! Er – how do I do that?

You can learn general planning guidelines from the next section. This is because the principles that govern essay planning lie behind all planning success.

> **Normally I don't have problems planning, but I'm finding one essay plan tricky. Can I just start writing?**
>
> In extremely rare cases, it may help to postpone planning. If you've tried planning some coursework and find yourself going round in circles, you may find greater inspiration by starting to write. You'll have to fiddle about with the structure afterwards, which is time-consuming and can be risky. Therefore, this isn't a good exam tactic, and generally not good practice.

Plan your essays

First, have a clear idea in your mind of the point of the exercise. Here are a few functions that essays perform, depending on subject and other contexts:

Essays: what's the point?

- Show understanding of key issues
- Offer in-depth analysis
- Argue a certain viewpoint

How can you make your essays achieve *all* the above aims? Simply by working your way through the following five key steps:

1 Interpret the question correctly
2 Develop your answer
3 Structure your answer
4 Work out your introduction
5 Work out your conclusion

The following sections take you through these steps one by one.

1 Interpret the question correctly

Start by working out what the question *asks you to do*. Be careful – this can be deceptive. For example, consider the differences between the following two look-alike questions:

Differentiate look-alike questions

Q1 'Animals today are slaves to humans.' Discuss.
Q2 'Animals should be slaves to humans.' Discuss.

The first question asks for a definition of slavery and an analysis of how closely the term applies to animals in the modern world. It asks whether animals have always been and will always be subjugated, with the implication that slavery is morally wrong and that therefore we should change our behaviour towards animals.

The second question focuses less on the definition of slavery, requesting instead an analysis of the differences between animals and humans. A good answer to this question would argue whether one species can justifiably subjugate another.

There is naturally some common ground between both questions, but the angle of approach is quite different. You can use the following techniques to steer yourself in the right direction:

①
Underline

- Underline key words within the question:

Q1 Animals <u>today</u> are <u>slaves</u> to humans. <u>Discuss</u>.
Q2 Animals <u>should</u> be <u>slaves</u> to humans. <u>Discuss</u>.

- Paraphrase the question:

②
Paraphrase

Q1 Is it true to say that, in the modern world, we exploit other animals as if they were our slaves?
Q2 Regardless of whether they do so or not, is it acceptable for humans to exploit animals? If so, on what basis? If not, why not?

2 Develop your answer

Once you're quite sure you understand the question, you're ready to work out your response. Some students like to plan this in detail; others find it restricts their thinking too much. If in doubt, err on the side of detail, particularly where you notice yourself writing cop-outs like 'etc.' or 'say how x happens'. This means you are instructing yourself to think *later*; but you must think *now*. Push through the pain barrier and decide exactly what you mean. Nudge the answers out of yourself with the following questions:

- Why?
- How?
- What causes this?

Ask questions
that trigger new
ideas

- What are the implications of this?
- Are there other examples?
- How could I back this up?

Once you force yourself to scrape the bottom of the barrel in this way, you will find that new ideas and associations spring to mind, enriching your work.

To plan coursework, give yourself ample space to insert extra notes between points. I start by sketching out a mindmap that I redraft in a linear, point-by-point style once I've decided what my

Make space for points (e.g. mindmap)

points are (see Chapter 4 for mindmapping guidelines). I rarely tackle introductions or conclusions until I've dealt with the bulk of the essay. This is because I find the beginning and ending easier to work out once I know the middle.

3 Structure your answer

Having developed your ideas, you now have to decide how to organise them so that they flow logically, one from the other. Normally, you would do this by working out what headings or groups your ideas fall into. In doing so, you will often find you face two choices:

Structure by block or by theme?

- A block structure, whereby you deal with topics in blocks, one at a time.
- A theme structure, whereby you deal with more than one topic at a time, under shared headings.

How can I give my coursework a good structure?

Put in some headings and subheadings that help to draw out the underlying themes in your work. They also give your reader a glimpse of the path your essay will take.

The document map function on your computer lists headings, which gives you a helpful bird's-eye view of your structure.

---

*Block = A   1
            2
            3
B   1
    2
    3*

*Theme = 1   A
             B
2   A
    B
3   A
    B*

For instance, think about the way this book is structured. Look at it as being one long essay about two main topics: coursework and exams. I could have chosen a block structure in which I dealt with coursework and exams in separate chapters and worked my way through point by point. Instead, I chose a thematic structure and focused on themes – each chapter deals with a different theme, as the chapter headings indicate. I considered how those themes applied to both coursework and exams. Why did I do that? Wouldn't it have been simpler to devote a section of my book to coursework and another to exams? Well, as you've probably gathered by now, coursework and exam preparation share much common thematic ground, and the attitudes and techniques behind coursework success also lie behind exam success.

This isn't to say that there is anything wrong with a block structure. If your topics don't have many themes in common, it's your best option. A block structure also boasts greater simplicity: instead of jumping back and forth from one topic to another, you start with one, which you consider from all angles, before moving on to the next.

4 Introduce by asking: 'Why bother?'

*Intros state
your purpose*

At school, you were probably taught to introduce your work by using the 'say what you're going to say' method. At higher levels this exercise can be a torment because the complexity of the subject doesn't make it amenable to a brief analysis. A more helpful approach is to reflect upon why you are embarking on your enterprise at all – in other words, outline your *purpose* in writing the essay. In this way your introduction can contain answers to the following hidden questions:

- What's the point of spending time on this?
- Why is this issue interesting?
- What's the relevance of the topic?
- Why did I choose this question?

Here are a few other introductory ideas:

Other tips

- Rephrase the question, explaining your interpretation of it. This tactic is particularly useful where you perceive some ambiguity in the question.
- Set the question in its historical/geographical/other relevant context.
- Always define words or ideas in the question that are subject to debate or that are specialist/technical terms.
- Quote, list facts, or outline the background to your piece.
- Give an outline map of the route you're going to take and justify your approach, particularly if you intend to narrow the question down.
- Introduce one or more key issues/questions.
- Give a relevant case study that leads gracefully to the point.
- State a provocative idea in an ordinary way.
- State an ordinary idea in a provocative way.

Do you want to let the cat out of the bag?

*Conclusions
can make clear
(but dull)
openers*

So far the ideas I've given you for your introductions don't give away your final answer. This enables you to build up to your conclusion and end with a flourish, which is ideal in arts subjects or other fields where a little drama has its place. However, you can take a different tack and state your conclusion in your opening paragraph, leaving the remainder of the essay to back it up. It's not quite so exciting to read, because the reader knows what's coming. Nonetheless, you may like this alternative. It has the benefit of clarity.

If you're worrying about what this approach would leave you to say in your conclusion, I'm sure you'll find enough ideas in paragraph 5 below.

Can I use 'I' in my written work?

It depends. In introspective subjects where subjectivity is valued (e.g. psychotherapy) you may actually be expected to use 'I'. In other fields, it may appear too personal.

A more academic alternative to 'I' is 'we', as it includes your reader's viewpoint, showing that you are aware of your audience.

If in doubt, ask your tutor, as it's important to use the appropriate register in your work. Whatever you use, be consistent.

---

5 Conclude by asking: 'So?'

Conclusions show the wider picture

At school, you might have satisfied your teachers by concluding with a summary (otherwise known as the 'say what you've just said' method). At higher levels, use the opportunity to look at your subject with a wider-angle lens, so that you give the reader a sense of *overview*. Ask yourself what meaning the subject has in the larger sense. For instance, if you trace the development of an important figure, be it in history, philosophy, English or science, your conclusion might reflect upon that person's contribution to the subject as a whole: think about what he or she changed, or failed to change. The conclusion is also an opportunity to show awareness of your own limitations – your answer can't be totally comprehensive at higher levels. Explain what you have had to miss out, and evaluate the impact on your essay of such omissions.

A few more pointers:

Other tips

- Answer the question! If you can't give a clear answer, say so and show what prohibits you from drawing a definite conclusion.
- Consider what may happen in the future – or what happened next.
- Does it throw light on the question to take a lateral view and mention other examples/systems/countries?

- Give your opinion, if relevant.
- State whatever is the accepted or current view on the question.
- Consider the implications of agreeing or disagreeing with the question: maybe it changes the way a situation should be interpreted, or maybe action needs to be taken.
- Quote, and explain why or how the quotation sums up your theme.
- Create a sense of completion by recalling an earlier idea.

Essay planning practice (if you want it)

You may not be confident about essay planning, so start by practising with easy topics – the technique is much the same whatever subject you tackle. Let's practise with the question from earlier in this chapter:

'Animals of today are slaves to humans.' Discuss.

Spend no more than half an hour planning your answer. When you've finished, read on.

At university level, there is rarely a perfect answer, so if you've taken a different tack from the one outlined in the next few pages, *A practice* don't worry. You could tackle this question from various angles, *essay plan* but the following pages offer some suggestions.

Ideas for an introduction

+ feedback
- Define slavery (this is a must).
- Outline why it matters whether humans treat animals as slaves. One argument could be that it is the sign of a civilised society that it treats its weakest members with respect. You could also use the 'animals are sentient beings' argument.
- Give the limitations of your field of enquiry: if you are narrowing the question down to the developed world – or even just the UK – justify your decision.
- List examples of animal abuse that show the question's validity.

Ideas for a main section

- Limit your answer to this century.
- Agree: food industry (battery farming, animal transportation, slaughter methods); animal testing (cosmetic vs medical); cloning; zoos; circuses; pets (caged birds).

- Disagree: food industry is changing (free-range, organic); protected species/habitats; animal welfare charities (RSPCA); laws (against animal testing, bear-baiting); animals redundant in modern agriculture, transport and warfare.
- Counterargue: if animals were not treated like slaves in the first place, such laws and charities need not exist.

I've given you broad outlines, but do make sure that your essay plan gives good details. Remember that the more specific you are, the more ideas will spring to mind. If you have problems developing your main points and your essays are always a bit too thin, try prompting yourself by writing your main point in a margin: this leaves ample space for your development, as illustrated in Table 6.1. This shows an argument (zoos have improved) followed by its counterargument (they still enslave animals). I've marked 'transport' and 'circus' with an asterisk to show you that they triggered more key arguments as I wrote, such as the trade in animals for their body parts and the use of animals for entertainment in circuses.

Table 6.1 Part of an essay plan

Main point	Backup and development (i.e. details, background, causes, effects, examples, illustrations, analogies, names, facts and figures, graphs, data, etc.)
Zoos have improved . . .	Initially created purely for benefit of humans. Animals = collectors' item. Many died in transport* or unsuitable conditions.
	Nowadays zoos preoccupied with animal welfare?
	• Replicate natural habitat (e.g. hide food) • Preserve endangered species (e.g. Gerald Durrell zoo) • Closing down, replaced by safari parks
. . . but still enslave animals	A gilded cage is still a cage (dolphin shows: animals, captive, must perform tricks – like circus*). Safari animals have space, but still captive.
	Evidence of suffering: animals don't reproduce easily (panda); boredom and frustration (wild cats).
	Purpose? Largely entertainment for kids. Money-spinner. No justification other than to preserve endangered species – circular argument (humans endangered animals in the first place).

Develop main points with good backup

Ideas for a conclusion

- Answer focuses on developed countries. Animals in western society have more legal rights, but animals in eastern society are less exploited by the pharmaceutical and food industries. A thorough examination of the problem worldwide might reveal that the more civilised a society the worse its animals fare.
- Animals are evidently slaves. They should be liberated – or not (this touches on the 'animals should be slaves' question analysed earlier).
- *More feedback* According to the Bible, it is acceptable for humans to sacrifice animals. Argue whether a 5000-year-old ethic excuses barbaric practice (bear-baiting, bullfighting) and more modern developments in animal exploitation (testing, circuses, zoos, the ivory trade).
- The implications of agreeing with the question are that we abuse our powers over animals and that such abuse reflects our abuse of the entire planet, threatening not only animal welfare but also our own children's survival.
- As society grows more civilised, minority groups – children, women, ethnic – are increasingly liberated. However, what are the chances of animals being liberated? Not great, given that (1) they can't voice their rights and (2) they belong to a different species. Therefore we don't have the same degree of empathy with them as with humans (an exception could be argued for cuddly animals).

Essay confidence

What did it feel like planning the above essay? Did you feel comfortable doing it or did you worry all the way? Was it awful reading my suggestions, because it made you feel bad about all the points you wished you had made? Did the whole idea of planning put you off so much that you evaded the exercise and skipped to this section?

'Essay' = 'just have a go!' *Essayer* in French means 'to try': when you write an essay, you could think of it as just 'having a go'. I suggest this because students can be terribly daunted by a notion that there is a perfect essay for every topic, and that they must produce a masterpiece or die. The truth is much kinder than that.

The limitations may not be yours

①
You can't
say it all

I can assure you that your essays will never be perfect at higher levels, because you haven't got the space to say everything that has been said or indeed could be said. Neither is this desirable: too much deference to others' views and you end up trying to include in your essay everyone else's ideas *but* yours. It's not just that you lack the time and word space to research all the experts. This isn't the point of the higher level essay, where your aim is to show that you are able to discriminate and sift material as you build your own ideas.

②
There isn't
much space

The essay format has its limitations: you can't satisfyingly boil down a complex subject into a few paragraphs and sentences. Students whose thought processes are well developed and well connected often find this frustrating, as they have reached a point where the depth of their knowledge and understanding about the questions they are set outgrows the essay format. A good analogy is to imagine you have to write a few thousand words on your life. You would have to be ruthless in choosing which aspects of your life to analyse and develop.

How can I get started easily on my coursework and exam essays?

Decide on a topic as early as possible, to give your unconscious mind time to develop ideas.

Sketch out immediately what you already know. In coursework, this helps to define and limit your areas of research. This sketch is the basis of your plan.

Write a pretend first paragraph to help you get going.

You can leave your introduction blank, starting with main points (even in an exam). Return to it later when, with hindsight, it will be easier to introduce your essay.

---

③
There are few
set answers

All in all, essay writing requires resilience at higher levels, since it isn't always satisfying to try and fit huge subjects into a relatively small structure. What's more, higher level questions lend themselves rather less to definite conclusions and simple answers, and rather more to hypotheses or further questions. Therefore, if you're stuck with your essays you're probably trying to do too much: pare down your arguments and pan out from a few basic principles, rather than trying to start from great heights where you may very well get lost.

Even in longer pieces, such as coursework essays, the best you can do is to give evidence that you have grasped the main issues, and that this knowledge has given you ideas with which to explore a few finer points. You may be dissatisfied with your final effort, and feel compelled to keep redrafting it; rest assured that, like revision, coursework is never really finished but abandoned.

④
You could keep redrafting for ever!

However, once you give up all hope of a masterpiece, life gets easier. You don't have to wade through volumes of academia before you put pen to paper yourself – not even for coursework. Here are some advantages you gain from trying *not* to write the perfect essay:

- You allow yourself to express your own ideas
- You make the most of what you know already

Aim for good enough

- You don't get tangled up in excessive background reading
- You get started
- You enjoy your work, as it grows more assertive and personal

Once you become self-assured in your ability despite its limitations, you will find that you dare to develop your own opinions. In the initial stages of higher education, students often feel they can't do what other academics do; they can only repeat,

Kick out intrusive thoughts at essay time

Be bold

or copy the great masters. Kick out intrusive thoughts about not being able to do what others do. You're still good enough to make your own mark, perhaps by boldly putting forward your own ideas, questioning other people's theories and drawing your own conclusions.

Have the bottle not to plagiarise

Plagiarism is the theft of intellectual property. A plagiariser takes other people's material – be it text, graphics, images or other printed matter – without stating its author and origin. This isn't always deliberate fraud: many students who plagiarise do so unwittingly.

Plagiarising backfires

It's vital that you make correct reference to your sources, because plagiarism is penalised at higher levels of education. Your markers will most probably have read everything you've read, even if you think it's terribly obscure and well disguised in your essay. Don't waste time trying to dress up a point as your own: refer to the point openly as someone else's and state whether you agree or disagree.

Acknowledge + compare/ contrast sources

You don't lose points by admitting that you got your ideas from an expert; in fact, you gain points if you show you can analyse these ideas and build on them, or compare them to other experts' ideas and show how they complement or contradict each other.

You may find it hard to distinguish between drawing inspiration from your reading, which isn't plagiarism, and, on the other hand, copying the essence of someone else's thoughts, which is. If you're not sure, ask your tutor, or look up the University of British Columbia's website on www.zoology.ubc.ca/bpg/plagiarism.htm.

Plagiarism website

This offers an in-depth explanation on the subject.

Low self-esteem

If you suffer from low academic self-esteem, you will almost certainly be tempted to plagiarise in your coursework. As an escape from the ordeal of thinking independently, the plagiariser takes refuge in research, feeling insecure about how much is out there that perhaps ought to be in the essay. Anyone who does lots of research is bound to come across terrific passages that it feels heartbreaking to leave unstolen. The plagiariser can't resist this temptation, as he or she is plagued by doubt: 'Why should I try to do my own thing which may never be as good as this?'

The plagiariser also fears the planning effort, which means coming face to face with his or her own limitations and inadequacies. It's daunting to imagine tackling university topics head-on; taking someone else's view seems like a much safer bet.

Dare to develop original ideas

Of course, learning *not* to defer to another's judgement is one essential purpose of education. If you can develop an original line of thought, you enjoy the greatest experience a higher level course may offer you.

An anti-plagiarism strategy

If you lean too heavily on other people's work, I suggest you organise yourself so as to make plagiarism nigh on impossible. You might like to try organising your background research well before you do any writing. Then, close your books and do nothing for weeks so that your unconscious has time to do some sifting for you. You'll remember the important points, which you can connect in a framework that is a creation of your own. Look up specific details when your writing is over.

Reference your sources

Now that I've persuaded you to confess your sources you may be wondering what the procedure is for doing so. The most established referencing system is the Harvard system, according to which sources are marked in the text by giving:

Harvard referencing

1 The author's name
2 The date of the relevant publication in brackets

All literature referred to is listed at the end of the essay under the heading 'References'.

Here's an example:

Anne Alvarez (1992) suggests that mothers function as 'alerters, arousers and enliveners' of their babies.

References
Alvarez, A. (1992) *Live Company*. London: Routledge.

Plan your oral presentations

Good preparation for presentations involves thinking about the point of the exercise. Ask yourself why you are being asked to present your ideas 'live'. It goes without saying that oral examinations test foreign language students on fluency; but for other subjects the answer to this question depends on your topic and, to some extent, on your personality. Certainly there are advantages you may gain from this style of assessment, such as the ability to:

Presentations
offer
opportunities

- Breathe life into your topic
- Discuss ideas with a degree of complexity possible in an oral context, particularly where a discussion may ensue
- Offer a personal approach
- Back up your ideas with illustrations, graphs or charts

Language orals

Oral presentations need careful preparation, because anything you say before an audience needs to be rehearsed. Seasoned actors would never dream of going live on stage without rehearsal, and they don't even speak their own words! If you're a foreign language student it's a good idea not only to prepare topic vocabulary but also a few words and expressions that enable you to hesitate naturally, as a native speaker would do (a good tip is to listen to the phrases politicians use in stalling difficult questions live on the media). Prepare also a range of questions you could ask your examiner, since you gain marks for simulating a spontaneous conversation in which you take the lead.

Here is some general advice for all presentations:

Planning tips

- Plan what you wish to say as you would plan an essay: introduce, develop and conclude (go back to essay planning guidelines earlier in this chapter). You can write your entire text out longhand, if you like, although this is by no means necessary as you will have to reduce it to note form anyway.
- Include in your introduction an outline of the duration and structure of your talk. Flag up the key topics you will cover, and briefly explain why. This is because people listening to a presentation often feel out of control. Once they know what to expect, they can relax and become more receptive.
- Make space for questions in your talk. For instance, throw in a line like 'Why is this the case?' Engage your audience by making them think of possible answers, even if you provide all the answers yourself.
- Picture your audience, to work out a suitable tone – formal or relaxed? How lively and entertaining can you be? Should you use specialised vocabulary, and if so will your audience expect it to be explained?
- Draw up a list of aids you might need: an overhead projector, coloured pens, illustrations or charts. Don't shy away from using these; they can lend interest to your talk. If you do use props, practise using them ahead of time so that you use them slickly.
- Always practise using a microphone if you have the opportunity.
- Anticipate questions and prepare some convincing answers.

Reduce your
presentations
to notes

Once you've worked out the content of your presentation, *reduce it to note form.* You must do this because your presentation will thrive on eye contact and a certain degree of spontaneity. The best lecturers reduce their notes to a handful of keywords; however, until you are experienced at this skill, I suggest the following approaches:

- Linear notes on A4 paper, with main points on the left-hand side of the page and detail on the right.
- Index cards, in sequence – each card contains a condensed paragraph.
- A mindmap.
- Keywords – each one reminds you of a paragraph of your text.

For my own presentations I prepare keywords and write out key links. This ensures I progress smoothly from one point to the next in the heat of the action.

Your final task is to practise speaking your presentation out loud. The object is to:

- Develop your own personal style. By rehearsing, you grow more comfortable with your material and find a natural way of delivering it.
- Work out timings. Once you're 'on stage' your internal clock may become unreliable, so write down a few time targets in select places on your notes, so that you can adjust your speed as required.

Rehearse
everything

- Practise using your notes/cards/mindmap/keywords.
- Practise presenting your material in spoken form. I recommend you either record yourself or ask a friend to give you honest feedback about the way you use your voice. Can you be heard from the back of the room where you will be giving your presentation? Are you using the microphone properly? Limit your hand gestures, make some eye contact with your audience, and above all, stand still.

You may dislike the notion of rehearsing your presentation. Do it anyway. You're probably just nervous and rehearsal will soothe your anxieties. If it doesn't, comfort yourself with the actors' adage that a poor dress rehearsal guarantees a good performance on the day.

Plan your vivas

Depending on your subject, you might expect to take a viva, or interview-style exam ('viva voce' means 'with the living voice' in Latin). In small departments, like botany for example, it may even be routine for all candidates to be interviewed. If you are selected for a viva, this will be for one of the following reasons:

Viva selection:
purposes

- Most commonly, to decide what grade boundary you fall into.
- To give you a chance to redeem a poor coursework or exam performance.
- To give you a chance to embellish a promising coursework or exam performance.
- In rare cases, to applaud your stunning exam result.
- To check the authenticity of your work.
- To use you as a benchmark against which to assess other candidates.

It makes sense to prepare your viva as fully as you can, particularly if you suspect one of the first three reasons applies to your situation. In addition to guidelines I've just given on oral presentations, here's some further advice:

- Revise the stronger points you might have shown in coursework or in an exam.

Prepare for
awkward
questions

- Consolidate weaknesses you think you might have shown in coursework or in an exam.
- Draw up a list of all the best and worst questions you can imagine the exam board asking you. Prepare your answers.
- Get a friend to test you and give you feedback on your performance, not just on the strength of your answers but also on the messages you convey through your body language and tone of voice. A humble-yet-confident style works best in these kinds of situation.

Plan your practicals

Practicals are nothing less than the foundation of all scientific and technical discovery. They usually involve skill acquisition, anatomical exploration or, most frequently, hypothesis-testing. These are not accomplished in a day and therefore, like all large undertakings, practical work needs to be planned to produce

Practicals
require
foresight

meaningful results in the time you have. It really pays to be patient and persistent in the initial preparatory stages.

Follow
instructions

Some practical work comes with step-by-step instructions. If so, scrutinising these before you start will help you spot problems ahead of time.

However, at other times you may be given very little guidance and be expected to do your own research and planning. It's possible that your tutors may overestimate your knowledge base and how much you understand the theoretical and technical aspects of the work, so if you're unsure of something, find it out.

Or ask

Use all your resources: you can usually get good advice from technical and academic staff on what *should* happen. Students in the year above are good for advice on what *actually* happens!

Being in control of your practical work doesn't just give you the benefit of better results but also helps you to enjoy the process. The following guidelines can help you sail through the process of planning, conducting and writing up your practical work.

More tips

- Start ahead of time. Practical work rarely goes to plan, so if you keep well ahead of schedule you give yourself time to rerun something if it goes wrong, as it notoriously does.
- Make sure that you understand what you are investigating, and why.
- Check the theoretical background: you need to grasp the under-lying science.
- Ask yourself whether your aims are realistic in the light of how much time you have; whether you need to travel; if you have access to the right equipment; and so on. Students planning their own work often overestimate what they are capable of, so if in doubt, keep it simple.
- You will almost always need statistical analysis of data. It makes sense to start by finding out what test you will be using so that you collect the appropriate kind and quantity of data for it.
- Choose an experimental method that will yield appropriate data. Check that you are capable of conducting this method – for instance, that you have access to all the necessary equipment.
- If you need to order equipment from technical staff be sure to order the right kind and quantity, and do it well in advance.
- Check that you fully understand the techniques that are used, and that you can implement them yourself. Does a technique have pitfalls? If so, try and practise it ahead of time.
- Use your time efficiently. For instance, with a little planning, you might be able to run more than one sample at once in order to get enough work done in the time available.

- A rainy spell, a failed experiment or faulty equipment can mean that you need twice as long as you imagined. Aim to get to the laboratory in the morning, not the afternoon. That way, you have enough time to deal with the unexpected before the building closes.
- Should anything begin to unravel, stop, take stock and salvage what you can. Resist the temptation to falsify or 'borrow' data to cover a failure or save time. If you ask staff for advice and show that you're trying to think your way out of a difficult situation they will usually be more than willing to help out. They've all done it!
- If you're sitting a practical exam, prepare by using the equipment before the day – or at least reading up on it – and running processes through your mind so that you know step by step what you are going to do. By anticipating various likely scenarios you can stay calm under pressure.
- When you write up your work, follow standard form and layout (ask tutors for full guidance). Ensure that your conclusions refer back to your original hypothesis and that they are justified by the statistical tests or results you have obtained.

Simple, really.

In a nutshell

At higher levels, you can never know everything about your subject. However, planning skills help you score points even with a little knowledge, because you can interpret questions correctly, make an educated guess, back up your arguments, develop your views, make your ideas flow and justify your conclusions.

Well, now you know how to do all that, we're ready to talk about your exams!

6 PLAN FOR SUCCESS

Intro	Main point ↓	Development ↓
	Why bother planning?	Exam repots Thinking : crucial Red/afts
1	Interpret	Accuracy lookalike questions : deceptive (eg animals + humans Q.)
2	Develop	State main point Develop it (detail, backup, causes + effects, examples, illustrations, analogies, names, facts + figures, graphs, data)
3	Structure	Cohesion Flow Block / Theme Intros + Concs.
	Essay plans	Practice : a model answer Limitations —— essay format ↘ huge subjects
	ʃ Vivas ʃ Practicals, Orals	Confidence vs plagiarism
Conc	So ?	If can argue, interpret, guess, justify → you're ready for exams !

7

Master your exams

- The value of exam technique
- Essay exams
- Multi-choice exams
- Orals
- Before and after

It ain't what you do, it's the way that you do it. That's what gets results.

Anon

This chapter offers in-depth exam technique

Having got this far, you now know everything that's worth knowing about revision, so you have almost all the strategies you need for success. What remains is for you to master your exams. The rest of this chapter offers all the skills you need for that purpose and talks you through the process, from the eve of your exams to the aftermath.

Absorb the advice in this chapter well before the day, so that you can give it a trial run in your exam preparation.

Exam success: fantasy vs reality

Here I am telling you to prepare, and yet it seems that plenty of students do shockingly little preparation for terrific results. What's their secret? Are they endowed with magic powers?

There's no magic behind success

No. Although it's true that some students have a greater knack for their subject than others, aptitude alone isn't enough to produce good results in exams at higher education levels.

Many good students would certainly like you to think they don't work, in order to make their excellent exam results appear doubly impressive. Others would rather be skinned alive than admit how much they care about their work. Some fear that their results may not match up to the high expectations they have of themselves, so to protect their image they spread the word that they haven't done a spot of revision. When these students get their results, everyone's jaw drops: 'How did you do that?' They shrug their shoulders, blush a little and mumble something about being lucky with the paper.

Aside from this category, there are a few students (not many) who really and truly don't prepare much for their exams, yet still manage to score excellent results. Yes, intelligence plays a part in their exam success, but that's not the only factor. Their success also comes from applying the study skills that you're learning from this book.

Lay to rest your fantasy of a 'superstudent' if you ever believed it. The fantasy is dangerous for two reasons. First, it may make you feel very depressed if you believe (as you should) that you can't get stunning exam results on no work. I've heard many students grumble despondently, 'Some people can, but I can't.' It's quite uplifting to realise that in fact there's no magic behind exam success.

The superstudent fantasy: dangers

The superstudent fantasy is particularly dangerous for those students who try to be superstudents themselves. To prove to themselves and others that they have supreme powers, these ambitious mortals put off working until the very last minute before their exams, when the harsh reality strikes them that they have set themselves an impossible goal.

Let's make it crystal clear. Exam success boils down to three factors:

- Innate ability (20 per cent)
- Good knowledge of the subject (30 per cent)
- Strong exam technique (50 per cent)

The percentages I've estimated give you a rough idea of how much each factor contributes to exam success. They also show the importance of exam technique. For all your revision, you still can't reproduce your notes as you might have done at school: you need to discriminate and think afresh. Exam technique helps you do that.

> **I've left it all too late. I can't prepare now – there isn't enough time!**
>
> You may be trying to convince yourself that it's too late. That way, you don't have to do any work!
>
> How much time have you got left? A month? A week? Well, you can do a lot of work in a week.
>
> Make the most of the time you have left by being strategic. Draw up your revision priorities and do plenty of exam practice using the guidance in this chapter. You'll boost your results and calm your anxiety by taking action now.

Fear is OK

Before you read on, a word about exam nerves. The correlation between confidence and exam success isn't as close as people imagine. Stress and insecurity can be excellent assets, making you more alert, decisive or careful. Just knowing that you have good exam technique will help you remain level-headed enough to cope well throughout.

The day before

Take the day off

My advice? Take the day off. The best use you can make of the day before your exam is to recharge your batteries and plan a good night's sleep. I have to be honest, though, and confess that the day before my own finals I simply couldn't help doing just a tiny bit of work, just to reassure myself that my brain was still working. I went over a few exam essay plans, which didn't improve my knowledge or understanding of the syllabus, but just set my mind at rest.

I admit I was weak and untrusting. If you can, try not to work at all. If like me you can't relax, then just do the bare minimum. In any case, you can certainly set your mind at rest by preparing your materials and clothes for the next day, and double-checking the exam location and times.

Here are some ideas of what *not* to do the day (and night) before:

Exam eve don'ts

- Work all day until you feel totally wiped out and can't concentrate any more
- Spend time with someone who talks non-stop about tomorrow's exams
- Eat junk food which makes you feel sluggish
- Get drunk

- Go clubbing (a friend of mine had his drink spiked at a party the night before his finals)
- Watch TV late into the night
- Take drugs or pills that guarantee grogginess the next day
- Share a bed with someone who snores

If, like me, you find it hard getting to sleep the night before, remind yourself that just lying down and resting does you some good. The techniques on page 50 in Chapter 2 beat counting sheep.

Before going in . . .

Eat

Focus on your well-being

If you're feeling tense, eating may be the last thing you want to do. However, for once I'd advise you not to listen to your body and get something healthy and nourishing inside you. Your brain is going to be busy for a long stretch of time, and for that it needs good fuel.

Breathe

Focus on your breathing whenever you get butterflies in your stomach. They will disappear and you will be able to calm yourself. Regular breathing introduces a meditative state of mind that helps you stay level-headed.

Keep your distance

I suggest you think about where you spend the time leading up to your exam. Aim to arrive early. Once there, you may find it helpful going for a brief walk on your own. Without others around you to distract you with their questions and advice, you are likely to be calmer and more focused on the task that lies ahead. Many students feel that conversations with other students just before going into the exam can make them feel inadequate, as everyone is tempted to list the topics they have revised and predict what's on the paper. Although it makes those who are talking feel better, those who are listening usually start to fret about their own revision, and fear that it doesn't match up.

If you do get into such conversations, remember that you're not expected to know everything about your subject. This fact is

No one does perfect revision

particularly true at higher levels of education, where syllabuses dwarf GCSE and A-level requirements. You may wish you had spent more time on this or that aspect of your course, but you also probably realise by now that academic work never gets finished – all you can do is abandon it at some point. The feeling that you should have learnt more is quite natural and suggests, if anything, that you are conscientious and likely to do well.

The essay exam

Writing essays in exam conditions takes a bit of technique. Let me guide you through the process.

Prepare your desk

Start by laying out writing materials and other relevant bits and pieces.

Place your watch

A word about your watch. Because good timekeeping is vital to exam success, I suggest you work with a clock face (rather than a digital) watch, to help you visualise time more easily. A clock face is helpful when you have to calculate timings. It also acts as a useful guide when you need to check that you are working at the right pace. Pictures are easier to remember than numbers: you will recall where the minute hand was when you last looked. Place your watch somewhere on your desk where it will catch your eye.

Examine your paper like a menu

Read the whole paper

When you read a menu in a restaurant, you want to be sure not to miss dishes. Turn all the pages of your exam paper to gain the same overview – in some exams you are given five minutes' reading time to do just that. Check that everything is as you expected. Make sure it's the right paper, and not your neighbour's (exam invigilators sometimes get the simplest things wrong!).

You will already know, from your exam syllabus and from past paper practice, what the exam format should be, but confirm to yourself what sections you must complete, the number of marks you gain for different types of task and what options you have in choosing questions. Pay attention to *all* instructions (such as 'Answer two questions from each section') as there can, occasionally, be slight changes from year to year.

> **What should I do if I run out of time?**
> Most marks are earned by making basic points. You need to elaborate to get extra marks. It's not worth the effort: you must use what time you have left to snatch up more basic marks in your next task.
> Wind up so that your ending isn't too abrupt. Point out what aspects of the topic you have not covered to show that you know the issues even though you haven't the time to develop them. You might be able to summarise, draw a quick diagram or jot down a list.
> With a watch and a timetable, running out of time is an unlikely scenario, by the way.

Keep your head whilst all about you are losing theirs

Take time to think

As you do all this, be prepared for the fact that students around you will already be starting to write. Let them do it and remind yourself to work at your own pace: an early start and a high word count don't spell exam success. You need time to read, understand and reflect. That means spending the first few minutes of the exam daring to do absolutely no writing at all.

Dare to spend the first minutes of your exam just reading and reflecting

This is particularly challenging because these moments are likely to feel very charged. Once you turn the cover page and look over the questions, you may feel compelled to start writing immediately. If you like the questions you may want to pour out your thoughts on them. If you find the questions difficult you may also be tempted to start writing, as an escape from having to think about the task.

This is one reason why past paper practice is so helpful – it gives you confidence and experience in organising your time.

Jot down your timings

You will know from your past exam experience how crucial it is to get your timings right. In case you had forgotten, let me remind you why:

Reasons to timetable

- To know how much time you can spend on each question. Obviously, you should devote proportionately more minutes to questions worth more marks (it's perhaps too obvious to say, for instance, that you should spend twice as long on questions worth twice as many marks).
- To make time to plan your answers before you write them out.
- To make time to check your answers.
- To give yourself margin for error.

All this is far too important to be left to chance, especially at higher levels, where you are handling a greater volume of knowledge than in A-level exams.

Timetabling examples

There are many ways of writing out an exam timetable, depending on what order you choose to plan, write and check. I shall give examples two examples, both based on a three-hour exam that starts at 2.00 p.m. and ends at 5.00 p.m. As you know, Jack and Chloe have contrasting styles, but let's say for the sake of argument that they have just spent 15 minutes going over the paper and choosing their three equally weighted questions.

Jack's timetable

Jack likes to plan, write and check, in that order.

Calculation
Time now: 2.15
Exam time remaining: 2 hours 45 minutes for 3 questions
= 55 minutes per question (i.e. 10 minutes to plan, 40 to write, 5 for margin and checking)

Timetable
Q1 2.15 Plan
2.25 Write
3.05 Check

Q2 3.10 Plan
3.20 Write
4.00 Check

Q3 4.05 Plan
4.15 Write
4.55 Check

Chloe's timetable

Unlike Jack, Chloe prefers to plan all her essays first. She also prefers to leave all her checking till last.

Calculation
Time now: 2.15
Exam time remaining: 2 hours 45 minutes for 3 questions
Subtract 15 minutes' margin and checking at the end
= 2 hours 30 minutes
= 50 minutes per question (i.e. 15 minutes to plan, 35 minutes to write)

Timetable
Plan   2.15 Q1
2.30 Q2
2.45 Q3

Write 3.00 Q1
3.35 Q2
4.10 Q3

Check 4.45 Q1
4.50 Q2
4.55 Q3

Be a little flexible

Your timetable may be yet another variation on the same theme. Just devise whatever schedule serves your purpose. Give yourself a few minutes' leeway with your timings if you need it. Some questions require more thought than others, so you may be totally justified in devoting slightly more time to one question than another. That's fine as long as you stay within secure time limits.

And now, choose your questions . . .

Choose good questions

As I said, Jack and Chloe spend 15 minutes reading and choosing questions. It may seem like a long time, but it's time well spent. A careful question selection sets you up for success.

What's the best way to spot good questions? There are two options. One is to look for favourites. That's fine if you know what questions you like. Otherwise, you can choose your questions by a process of elimination, as with multiple-choice questions (see page 162). This helps you narrow down your options if you're not sure which questions you prefer. Once your options are narrowed, you can reflect in depth on what choices you have left, and discard what you like least. Here's a step-by-step guide:

How to pick the best exam questions

e.g. by elimination

1 *Eliminate irrelevant topics (such as the ones which are off your syllabus).*

2 *Paraphrase remaining questions. By paraphrasing, you make an in-depth effort to understand what each question is asking.*

3 *Eliminate again.*

4 *Draw up mini-plans for remaining questions. To help you make the best choice between questions within your range, jot down a few key points in answer to each, as you would if you were making an outline of a plan. By reflecting in this way on each question, its relative merits and drawbacks should become clear.*

Easy questions aren't always best

It's all very well knowing how to make your selection once you have certain criteria in mind, but what, exactly, should you be looking for in a question? Curiously enough, you should not necessarily be looking for easy questions. Easy questions sometimes encourage students to regurgitate their notes. The result is something misshapen, that follows the structure of the notes, rather than that directed by the question. Ideally, you want to choose topics that you feel confident you can tackle, but which are nonetheless interesting and make you think afresh. In deciding what questions are most suitable, I suggest you bear in mind the following two proverbs:

- *Nothing ventured, nothing gained.* A familiar question may tempt you to try and reproduce former essays. However, this doesn't guarantee a good result. Your rehashed answer isn't likely to be lively and engaging (particularly in an arts subject). It may even be irrelevant: as explained in Chapter 6 (pages 128–9) a word's difference in a question can require an answer with a totally new slant. This can be particularly hard to perform if a former essay is very present in your mind, so in such cases it's usually best to choose an entirely different question.

- *Handsome is as handsome does.* Exam questions can be deceptive. A suitable question may appear unsuitable if it's couched in terms you don't immediately grasp. A question with instant appeal may, upon closer inspection, turn out to be beyond your range. It's usually worth thinking twice before following easy choices. Conversely, it may be worth giving special consideration to questions that appear difficult. These could offer you more scope than you initially imagined.

. . . or choose later

So far I've implied that you have to choose all your questions first. Here are the advantages of this approach:

Choose questions in advance . . .
- You have more time to prepare your answers. Once you choose your questions, you trigger an unconscious process of planning, sorting and making connections.
- It makes it easier to recall useful material and gain a good overview of the issues before you start writing.

However, you may prefer to choose the first question and answer that in full before you make further choices. This approach has the following advantages:

. . . or as you go along
- You warm up before making more decisions.
- You gain a sense of completion by finishing one question before starting another.
- In situations where you suspect two questions might overlap a little, you have a chance to reflect thoroughly on the first before committing yourself to the second.

Plan!

Even if, somehow, you managed to get through your A-levels without planning your exam essays, you will do yourself a monumental favour by making time to plan in your higher level exams. If you're not sure how to plan, refer back to Chapter 6 and practise planning until you feel secure with the technique.

Your past paper practice should help you to see how much time you can devote to planning. This depends on the pace at which

1 part planning to 3 parts writing

you write, but as a rough guide aim for one part planning to three parts writing. For instance, if you have one hour per question, you can spend 15 minutes of each hour on your plans. Watch the clock as you plan, and stick to your timetable.

How can I avoid leaving out questions and parts of questions by mistake?

Ring the questions you must answer, and cross them off when you've completed them.

To ensure you answer all parts of the questions, underline every task – for instance, the following question can be divided into three tasks:

'Outline the <u>problem</u> and give a <u>solution</u>. How could this solution be <u>implemented</u>?'

Cross off each completed task.

Two ways of planning

①
Plan ⎱
Write ⎰
Plan ⎱
Write ⎰
②
Plan ⎱
Plan ⎰
Write ⎱
Write ⎰

Most students do what Jack does and alternate planning and writing. It's a perfectly sound and logical approach – they plan the first question and write it out, then do the same with the next question, and so on.

My personal preference is to do what Chloe does and plan all my questions first, before writing anything out. Although this approach may appear a little unnatural, it has certain advantages:

- It engages your thought processes right from the start. By planning all your questions first, you trigger off ideas and associations that have time to mature before you start writing. This is particularly helpful in arts subjects where questions can be open-ended.
- It protects you from poor question choices. By planning your answers first you have the flexibility to reconsider your choices, and to swap one question for another without wasting writing time.

If you like this approach, you really must practise it in timed conditions at home before attempting it in the exam. Here are two reasons why:

- Putting off writing until all your plans are finished takes confidence and experience. Your plans could take an hour to complete in all. By this time, many other students in the exam room will probably have been writing for 45 minutes, which can be unnerving unless you know what you're doing.
- You also need to switch quickly from one plan to another, and then to engage again with each plan in turn as you write out your answers. In other words, you need to get slick at gear-changing.

What should I do if I find all the questions hard?

With good revision, this is unlikely to happen. The following steps should help:

1 Reassure yourself that challenging questions offer a great opportunity to think afresh, producing engaging and lively answers.
2 Outline your answers to all questions, starting with the easiest. This should trigger ideas and associations.
3 Return to your outlines and consolidate them with these new insights.
4 Start writing when your planning time is up.
5 Keep a strict eye on the time throughout.

Get easy questions out of the way . . . or not

Provided you number your questions clearly, you don't have to follow the order of the paper (unless instructed otherwise). You can start wherever you like.

Tackling easy questions first has the following advantages:

Advantages of tackling easy questions first

- You make good progress in the early part of your exam, creating a satisfying momentum.
- By the time you get to the more difficult questions you feel mentally warmed up.
- You quickly clock up easy marks.
- You have time to gather your thoughts for the more challenging final questions, and may find you have better recall and more ideas when you get to them.

Alternatively...

On the other hand, you might like to get a difficult job over and done with straight away, so as to stop worrying about it. In that case, start with a difficult question – you don't necessarily have to complete it. Once you start drawing up a plan for it, you may find it turns out to be easier than you first imagined. At any rate, you may feel able to move on to easy questions, returning to the first with possibly more insight.

If you don't want to chop and change like that, and prefer to finish your plan and write your answer out while it's still fresh in your mind, then do so. Just keep a strict eye on the time when occupied with a difficult task, and refrain from writing anything out in full until you're quite sure of what you want to say.

Keep to the point

Scoring points in an exam means answering the question in every paragraph you write. There's no reward for straying from the relevant issues, even if you would prefer to write about something else.

It's worth thinking about the main reasons why students digress in exams:

Why students digress

- They misread the question. This is usually because they rush their reading of the paper, or ignore certain words in the question.
- They don't discriminate. They get over-involved in their own knowledge and reproduce old notes instead of thinking afresh.
- They get tired. As the exam progresses they start to lose their focus.
- They try to fill up empty space. This may be because they have chosen an inappropriate question or because the quality of their revision is at fault. Either way, they run out of ideas and don't dare make an educated guess, so they write about irrelevant issues instead.

If past exam experience suggests that you are susceptible to these types of difficulty, re-read the planning advice in Chapter 6 to ensure you interpret and answer questions properly. Here are some additional guidelines:

Tips to avoid digression

- Take extra care to interpret the question correctly. Read it slowly, over and over again. Paraphrase it; by writing the question in your own words, you make an effort to understand it clearly (your paraphrase may come in handy if you need to fill out your introductory paragraph).
- Be ruthless: you are a slave to the question, the whole question, and nothing but the question. Discard irrelevant material as

you plan. Once you get to the writing stage, look back at the question every time you start a fresh paragraph, to hold it in your mind.

- Expand and develop. If you have word space to fill, resist the temptation to veer off into secondary issues. Fill the gaps with common sense and relevant details, by expanding your ideas and going into more depth. Asking yourself questions like 'How?', 'Why?', 'In what way?' or even 'So what?' can help you make an educated guess (see planning guidelines in Chapter 6).

What if I'm not sure if I'm digressing or not?

Reject material only when you know you are digressing. If you're not sure whether a point is relevant to the question, include it to be on the safe side, but be brief.

Make space for hindsight

However good your planning, certain sections of your answer may be difficult for you to write without the benefit of hindsight. Just leave blank spaces, write the rest of your answer and fill the gaps later (obviously this means hazarding a guess as to how many lines you're likely to need). For instance, when I sat my finals, I used to hold off writing my introduction until I'd filled out the main points of my essay.

Leave blanks –
fill in later

It's not a bad idea to miss a line between paragraphs in any case, in order to give yourself space for easy insertion of new ideas.

Assume you know enough

Most students start planning and writing their answers without much awareness of their state of mind – yet their result largely depends on their attitude. If they carry an inner conviction that they can do good work, they automatically free up their thinking. If, on the other hand, they adopt the view that they are relatively incompetent and ignorant, their thinking processes become restricted by pessimism.

Pessimism can also be a natural response to difficult patches in the exam. Your first reaction may be a powerful sinking feeling that you don't know the answer. Ignore the feeling: it's your chatter-box, as you'll know if you've read Chapter 1 (see page 24). The chances are that you do know enough to answer the question, but you just need time to think.

Positive
thinking frees
up ideas

Pay attention to your mood throughout the exam. As time progresses you may become increasingly careless or despondent; if so, return to the principle that you can make the most of your exams with a little positivity. Try assuming knowledge rather than ignorance, to foster an attitude that helps you score points. Taking a break helps . . .

Take mini-breaks

Many students find that their concentration dips after about 40 minutes in an exam. Look around the exam room and you'll see students gazing blankly into the distance, chewing their pens, doodling or sitting back and yawning. Your mind will stray whether you like it or not, so you might as well be calling the shots.

Just a few seconds off can be sufficient to refresh your mind and keep you focused on answering the question. Here are the advantages of taking time out:

- You will probably *save* time. If you don't give yourself breaks you'll be prone to lapses of concentration that can creep up on you without you noticing. Mini-breaks can make you more efficient in the long run.

Breaks refresh mind + mood

- You may even be inspired. By allowing your conscious mind to rest, you give your unconscious mind more free rein (as when you're asleep and start to dream). This can give you a chance to do some spontaneous free association, and you may well emerge from your daydream mentally refreshed and enlightened.
- You will see issues more clearly. Your mini-break will offer you a better overview of your subject.
- You will stay level-headed. Mini-breaks can take the heat out of your exam. Students who don't take time off often report becoming irritable and impatient. They may feel compelled to rush their work and hang the consequences. By making yourself stop at regular intervals you can create an experience of exams that is relatively calm.

It's entirely up to you how you decide to break in the exam. I suggest you punctuate your work with short but frequent intervals during which you let yourself daydream. You'll thank me.

Can I take a break outside the exam room?

You can leave if you need the toilet or want some fresh air. An invigilator will accompany you.

To check or not to check

Some students resist checking their work. They hate reading it over for fear of finding mistakes: there isn't time to make changes, they argue, so why bother?

Good checking boosts marks

This argument doesn't really hold water. Checking time should be built into your exam timetable. It's worth it: by weeding out the inevitable errors that occur under exam conditions, the chances are that you can gain many extra marks.

A student might be reluctant to check where past experience suggests he or she never finds mistakes – or even worse, *adds* errors instead of removing them. If that's your experience, give yourself extra checking time so that you can be more thorough, and double- or triple-check where necessary.

In any case, checking at higher levels is a skill, and you need to practise it before your exam. You need to get used to putting yourself in the examiner's shoes and inspecting your work quite critically. It's easy to imagine you're checking when in fact you're simply glancing approvingly over the pages and missing mistakes. When I check my work I take the attitude that it's bound to contain imperfections and that I'm going to hunt them down.

Rather than trying to check everything at once, I also suggest you adopt a point-by-point approach, which can help you stay focused. The following guidelines should help you make the most of the exercise:

Checking tips

1 Look quickly over your paper to ensure everything is laid out as instructed. Look at it from the point of view of the examiner. Are the questions and pages numbered properly? Is your layout clear?

2 Look again a little more closely to see if you can spot illegible words. Examiners are normally adept at reading difficult scripts, but it's still worth trying to put yourself in the examiner's shoes and rewriting scruffy bits – there are bound to be some.

3 Now read your work over, looking out for spelling mistakes and deficiencies in style. Your expression should be intelligible; more than that, your phrasing needs to be elegant if you are in a language exam, so add punctuation that improves the flow of your sentences. If your sentences or paragraphs are too long, insert breaks using this symbol: ⌐

4 Check the finer points with a short checklist. In foreign language exams, for instance, it's often helpful to look out for typical grammatical errors. (For instance, accents must be included, verbs and adjectives must agree, nouns must have the right gender. In some Latin-based languages you can work out

many genders by checking suffixes.) In subjects where you need to show theoretical understanding, check that you have remembered to give key arguments and references and that your calculations, figures, dates and illustrative material are accurate.

5 Checking your work gives you an overview of your answers. You may realise that you've missed something out which you don't have time to add. In this case, mention what you would have liked to develop further.

Dear Mr Examiner, I just wanted you to know . . .

Don't beg for mercy

You may feel an urge to scribble a note to the examiner begging for leniency. Resist it. Tear stains and bank notes have been tried before, and they don't work. There's no point in writing that you feel awful, didn't sleep properly and think you're getting flu. If you have a learning difficulty, such as dyslexia, or if English isn't your first language, make sure you arrange for special provisions well ahead of the exam (see Appendix 5).

The last shall be first

Stay till the end

I don't advise handing in your paper until you're completely satis-fied with it or you're told to stop writing. People often start walking out halfway through the exam. You may feel foolish for staying behind, but look up and remind yourself of the Bible's last word on exam technique.

The multiple-choice exam

It's usually worth tackling the multiple-choice section of your papers first. This gives you time to think about your answers, and maybe make valuable changes before handing in your paper. Remember to timetable your multiple-choice as you would any other exam paper.

Practise multiple-choice technique

Multiple-choice questions follow the same format: the first part, or 'stem', is a statement followed by various alternatives; your task is to select one or more viable alternatives. You need to be extremely secure about your definitions in your preparation for these tests. Some of the alternative answers provided may be 'distracters' – misleading answers devised to catch out candidates whose grasp of theory is a little vague or confused. Proceed by elimination:

1 Read the entire paper quickly but carefully, marking answers that you know to be correct.
2 You are left with questions on which you have doubts. Cross out alternatives you know to be incorrect. This may give you the answer.

Eliminate 3 If you're still undecided, mark the question so that you can
wrong return to it later, hopefully with more hindsight.
alternatives 4 If you're still undecided, make a guess, checking first that there are no penalties for wrong answers. If there are such penalties, leave a blank.

In addition, the following guidelines should help you choose correct answers:

Other tips • Scrutinise every question instruction. For instance, there is an enormous difference between choosing the 'correct answer' and choosing the '*most* correct answer'. Underlining keywords of this kind may help.
• Thirty per cent of students score better by working out their own responses to stems before they read the alternatives on offer.
• In cases where all alternatives appear to be correct, the stem will give away what criteria you should use to help you discriminate. Every word in the stem matters: pay attention to keywords like 'always', 'sometimes' and 'never' which ask for absolutes. Some of the alternatives may not be correct in that restricted sense.
• Some stems test your logic with sequences of negatives, such as 'It's not uncommon to misunderstand . . . ' Turning these carefully into positives may help you think more clearly: 'It's common to misunderstand . . . '.
• Re-read the stem as you go through each alternative, to help you assess which one best fits the stem. At the very least, grammatical inconsistencies between stem and alternative strongly suggest a mismatch.
• In framing your final decision it helps to be suspicious of alternatives offering extremes (figures that are highest or lowest, for instance). These are often incorrect.
• In humanities and social science, steer clear of absolutes: very rarely is something entirely the case, or completely true.
• If in doubt, a correct answer may well be one which offers a range of possibilities, such as 'All of the above' – particularly if you know the majority of alternatives to be correct.

The oral exam

Most students in this situation feel quite nervous – this is normal and can be overcome by paying attention to your breathing. You could also try imagining that you are in a glass bubble that protects you from your audience and the outside world. Once you start talking your nerves will disappear and you may even start to enjoy yourself, if you have prepared well (see Chapter 6).

Visualise a protective glass bubble

Warm up

If you're taking a language oral, it's a good idea to immerse yourself in your target language before going on – for instance, it might be feasible to tune into a foreign radio station before your exam, to help you warm up. Remember that you must take control of the oral (and not just respond to the examiner), so screw up your courage to ask questions and show spirit. Here are some additional tips for all oral exams:

* Take a small bottle of tepid water to relax your throat. You can drink during your presentation, if necessary.
* Keep focusing on your breathing – this is the best way to stay calm.
* Take your time when you speak.

Don't be put off by your audience

People listening to you are likely to have been through the same process, and know exactly how you feel. If they're curiously expressionless it's probably because they're listening; even if they're frowning or look critical, it might be that they're just concentrating. It's usually a good idea to make a bit of eye contact with your audience. This goes without saying for students taking vivas, who need to try and gauge from their interviewers' cues whether to abandon or pursue a point.

Because oral exams put you on the spot, give yourself time to think. Even a few extra seconds can help you formulate a better sentence, or check that you are sticking to your planned timings. If you get a question you didn't expect, give it enough thought before you reply. Instead of 'Um', say something more erudite, like 'That's an interesting question – let me see now . . . '. People are normally quite happy to see you reflect before you speak.

Think on the spot

Just after the exam

You may be flooded with emotion as you walk out. Let the feeling pass. A surge of elation or depression is natural at this point and

Don't prejudge the results

may persist for weeks. Many students convince themselves that they have failed. Don't. You only know how you performed when you see your results.

It's entirely up to you how you spend your time after the exam. Most people recommend that students go into isolation, but you might long for the company of friends, to discuss the issues that came up and satisfy your curiosity about their views on the paper.

Post-mortems: pros + cons

Going for a drink after the exam may be a companiable thing to do. Talking to other students may even give you information that could be useful for your next paper, especially if certain topics overlap.

Just be aware of the risks: a discussion which dissects what you did or didn't put in your answer can make you worry about having done badly, missed out key points, forgotten references, or more. You may imagine you misunderstood the questions. If this happens, bear in mind that you are probably worrying unnecessarily. Quite apart from the fact that it may be the other person who is at fault and not you, your paper might still be perfectly good. Your answer might have certain strengths that you aren't aware of at the time.

By all means avoid those infamous post-mortems if your past experience tells you they do you more harm than good. Your priority is, after all, to turn your thoughts to your next paper.

 # So this is goodbye . . .

I hope you feel confident about your exams now that you've finished this chapter. Even if you follow only half the advice in this book, you will tackle them well.

Your *attitude* towards them counts more than anything. Exams are almost universally regarded as an evil, but you don't have to look upon them that way. As one of the world's greatest intellectuals pointed out, 'There is nothing either good or bad, but thinking makes it so'. Shakespeare, of course.

So, think of exams as a positive challenge. They summon you to develop a perspective on your life, look after your health, time-table, strategise, summarise, prioritise, discriminate and plan. These are all constructive goals that will serve you well beyond your exam days.

But perhaps the most profound and inspiring command of higher level exams is that you build your mind, by expanding your powers of thought to ever-increasing heights.

Congratulations for getting this far; I hope you've enjoyed improving your work. You now have everything it takes to make a success of your exams.

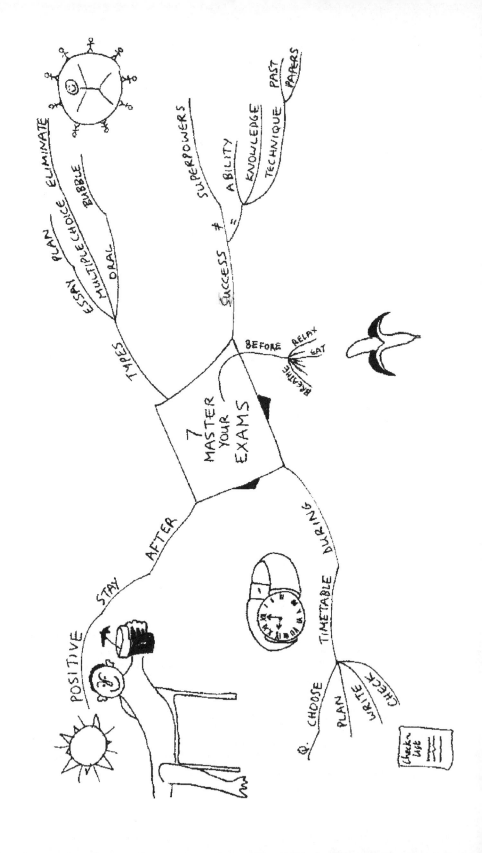

Part III

Testimonials

A word of explanation

My work as a study skills counsellor means that many students talk to me in total honesty about the pressures they are undergoing. I am privileged in this respect. Rarely do students talk candidly about their experiences. Often I get to hear stories that they wouldn't dream of telling anyone else – not even close friends and family.

Why the silence? Students are usually embarrassed about their failings because they imagine everyone else to be doing better. That's understandable, given that being a student means becoming prey to other people's judgements and criticisms. The more other people know about your weak spots, the more they can undermine you. So one reason why students don't talk about their difficulties is to avoid getting hurt and put down. Unfortunately this also makes for a lonely life. Some of the testimonials I have chosen depict that terrible isolation.

Another cause of silence can be immaturity: many students go to college straight from school, having very little real life experience or self-awareness. This makes it hard for them to put their finger on what's going wrong, let alone explain it coherently to anyone else.

The accounts I've collected show what it can really feel like to be a student. I was particularly interested in testimonials depicting very typical study difficulties. Some of the students who contacted me were still studying at the time, and some only wrote or phoned once or twice, so I can't always tell you how their stories ended. Other people I spoke to had finished their studies, so in their case, you have a more complete picture of those factors that turned out to be most instrumental in contributing to their successes and failures.

Put together, these accounts show – reassuringly – how unconnected the progression can be from academic success to personal or career satisfaction. Often, a bumpy ride can be just as effective as a smooth one in launching a satisfying career. Note that I don't know how happy and fulfilled my testimonial subjects feel in other aspects of their lives, so I wouldn't promote them to you as wholesale models of success – merely as evidence of the many viable approaches and outcomes that exist when tackling revision and exams.

My aim is to offer a range of personal experiences from which you can take heart. The more you can know about how others coped or didn't cope, the more comforted, warned, informed and inspired you can be in what can be quite literally the most testing time in your life.

On a practical note, where I felt a need to protect people's anonymity, I have changed names and details.

If you feel you would like to write to me in confidence about your own experiences, you can email testimonials@openup.co.uk. I will be glad to read what you have to say: everything I write is informed by what students tell me.

Rob: pulled down by family depression

Rob contacted me in the summer of 2004, aged 20, having recently failed to sit his second year university exams. Current figures suggest that one in ten students now quits university after the first year, so Rob is not alone in having problems at this juncture. His testimonial expresses, in concentrated form, the difficulties many students can face when their identities have not yet been fully formed.

I have good memories of doing GCSEs because I did subjects that I enjoyed. But taking A-levels started me thinking that there are winners and losers, and that I had to be a winner, which changed my objective from learning for the love of it to getting the best grades. I got straight As.

By the time I came to choose my university subjects, I was desperate for success. I always wanted to be a photographer and I had entered various competitions but never won anything. I decided I'd make money instead, as a way of compensating for not achieving my dreams. I think it was my way of expressing my anger with a world that had not rewarded my efforts. I didn't believe I could do what I wanted with my life. So I picked Law, in a calculating way. If I'd been wiser I might have put myself down for a subject I was more interested in, like Philosophy or Psychology.

My first year at university was OK because everything was so different. Law was new, so studying wasn't too boring – also living in halls meant that I worked when my room-mate worked, and in the evenings I went out. Looking back on it, socialising kept me going by relaxing me and reassuring me that things were fine. But I hated revising for the first year exams. I nearly dropped out. In the end I got through it partly because my parents encouraged me and my dad helped me with some of the subjects he knew a bit about.

I really dreaded going back for my second year. By then I was living at home and commuting to the campus. That was exhausting, and took up so much study time. I thought I ought to work hard and get good grades but my interest in the subject was evaporating.

In the first term of my second year I managed to hand in all my assignments on time, just, and got glowing reports – one tutor encouraged me to do an MA in his subject. No one realised that I was just scraping by, doing the bare minimum and leaving everything to the last minute. I knew I was losing my grip. In Law you have to learn hundreds of case studies and I kept vowing to catch up. But the more the work accumulated, the less I could get started.

I resolved to catch up over the Christmas holidays. But the first week went by. . . My dad was suffering from depression, so he couldn't give me support and the atmosphere at home wasn't conducive to work. I read your book over the vacation, which made me feel good while I was reading it (at least I was reading something!). I devised a timetable to catch up on the previous term's work and prepare for the forthcoming term – my idea was to reward myself on days when I'd done even a bit of studying. Each week I wrote out lists of aims and positive ideas from your book. None of it worked. I wasn't interested, every day seemed dull, there was nothing to look forward to, I didn't see the point of getting out of bed. By the third week I was smoking dope every evening to recover from the day. I had this notion that I could turn myself into someone who got up at eight, started work at nine, took an hour off for lunch and then carried on working till six. Instead, I was going to bed late after spending hours on the computer looking like I was working but in reality just surfing the net or playing computer games. So the next day I'd be getting up late and feeling groggy from having smoked so much the night before. Then I wouldn't be able to work until the afternoon, by which time I couldn't see the point. My parents told me I should treat my studies like a day job and work those kinds of hours. Every time I looked at my dad he seemed disappointed in me, and that made me very worried. I told myself I would work in the Easter holidays.

I spent the second term of my second year like a zombie, still getting by on dope, not really caring that I wasn't working, just setting my sights on surviving each day. That was difficult enough. I sat in on classes that didn't mean anything to me and went to the odd lecture to reassure people that I was working. My parents thought I was scraping by but by the second week I had stopped handing in assignments. Opening a book was too scary because it showed up how much work I had to do. I stopped seeing friends because they kept going on about work. I told one that I hadn't done any reading. He was really shocked, and asked what I did with my time, which made me feel awful. I went to see someone for one-on-one study support but it didn't help – I just came out feeling guilty because I knew I wouldn't do the tasks I was set. My exams came and went, and I didn't sit them. It felt almost good not to go.

That's not to say that the year was a waste of time. I learnt a lot about myself. I used to think that I could deaden myself to the world. Now I know I have to be inspired and excited about my work, to feel that I am doing something of real significance every day.

Rob's account illustrates how chronic family problems such as parental depression can sometimes inhibit otherwise capable students. He only mentions his father's problem once, in passing, because he doesn't realise how much it affected his own performance. But it's most likely that his academic struggles arose from his own depressive state, triggered by the depressive nature of his family set-up.

One depressive tendency is the need to be very special. Rob expresses a compulsion to win competitions, earn top whack or dazzle with good grades. Even at the end of his testimony, he still thinks he will be all right as long as he is constantly inspired and excited. Although he has learnt from his experiences that he needs to do something he enjoys, he still puts himself under a tremendous amount of pressure to be exalted on a daily basis. Rob hasn't been taught a realistic approach to life.

Nor has he learnt to handle failure. When Rob met with rejection in his photography competitions, he reacted in typical depressive fashion by turning his anger in on himself. His instinct, again and again, was to punish himself cruelly, by killing off what he loved in life and plotting a destiny calculated to turn him into a dead man, a money-earning zombie. It would have been good if someone had slipped him Richard Layard's book (see Chapter 1), which might have helped him to see that high salaries don't generate happiness.

Of course, repressed feelings eventually come bubbling up to the surface, which explains why Rob struggled to revise in his first year, despite his promising academic start. A sudden revision crisis is quite typical of students who need to be doing something different, but people around them often overlook this signal and instead, encourage perseverance. It looks as if Rob's parents fell into this particular trap.

So, with their help, Rob passed his first year exams. However, since nothing had been resolved, his struggle intensified in his second year. This is when he turned to my book. Study techniques often appeal to vulnerable people like Rob in that they promise structure, but Rob's overriding need was for a healthy (not depressed) parent figure who could show him a way forward. Deprived of this, Rob grabbed at substitutes such as time management, positive affirmations and lists of good intentions. But because these failed to address his inner needs, they didn't work. Worse, they made him feel like more of a failure, compounding his guilt. People like Rob often think of guilt as a spur to work. In small doses, it can be, but usually the guiltier people feel, the more they want to flee the workload.

It would have helped if someone non-judgemental could have explained to Rob that his escapist tendencies, towards displacement activities and dope smoking, sprung from a healthy enough instinct to find inner peace. He was just going about it the wrong way.

Rob might have stopped all this self-recrimination if he could have spotted the connection between his inability to work and his family problems. It's unfortunate that he picked a friend to confide in who had a very disapproving reaction. Things might have been different had the friend said something more interested like, 'I wonder why you're finding it so hard to work?' Rob's parents also unwittingly triggered more crippling guilt by suggesting that he work really quite impractical hours. Studying is much more intensive than the average nine-to-five routine, and emotionally much more demanding. The most Rob could have managed at his lowest ebb would have been a few hours a day.

The main reason why so many students today quit university is thought to be because they don't like the course they are on. As Rob points out, the fact that he dropped out of his exams may not be a bad thing. Paradoxically, it offers him a valuable opportunity to rethink. He is young and still learning: his failure gives him a far better chance of finding fulfilment than before. He could switch subjects and/or pursue his interest in photography. He could get a job to take the pressure off him. But above all, Rob now needs psychological support, to extricate himself from the cloying depression in his family, develop a more independent identity and so make better life choices.

Frederic: lateral thinking, success and the snowball effect

Frederic graduated from Oxford University in 2003 with a degree in Japanese. He now enjoys a career as a fashion and portrait photographer, which his studies unexpectedly launched. His testimony offers a refreshing antidote to the 'either-or' mentality that often so plagues young people who have a passion they'd love to pursue without necessarily forgoing a degree.

I'm Swiss-French and I grew up in Geneva. Although they didn't speak English themselves, my forward-thinking parents sent me to the International School to learn English. I made mostly Japanese friends there, and thought of Japan as an amazing place.

I wanted to study Japanese at university so that I could learn the language I had wanted to speak for so long. I also figured that a BA in Japanese could be extremely useful. My school had already sent some pupils to Oxford, so I thought I'd try too and I selected a college that I heard had its own Japanese tutor. At interview, I had to demonstrate linguistic abilities (although I couldn't speak any Japanese, I had French, English and some German from school), plus enthusiasm and motivation. It helped that my dad had been kind enough to send me to Japan for a week on my own, the summer before I applied. I was the first in my family to go to university.

I had always loved painting. At school I had spent a lot of time in the art room, but once I got into university I found learning Japanese so demanding that it left me no time to pursue my passion for art. I needed a quicker way of producing images. That's when a friend introduced me to the college darkroom. Photography suited my independent nature: I could go to the darkroom without needing to ask anyone for help and just build my skills from experience. To make all those darkroom hours more productive, I kept playing back recordings of myself reading out sentences from my Japanese textbook. The drill worked – my Japanese was improving, and so was my photography.

At Oxford you meet many passionate people from all backgrounds, and that opened up possibilities: I joined the photographic society, which I eventually ran for a year; I got friends to model for me; I approached students involved in student magazines or drama productions, and offered my services for free. It was a financial burden but I was willing to do it for the experience. Then a rugby team student calendar that I shot got national coverage, and I got paid for my photos, which is when I saw how photography could become lucrative. I got a few lucky breaks like that in the first few years.

Everything I learnt at Oxford came together in my fourth year, my year out in Tokyo. I'd already sent off my best prints together to 50 Japanese magazines: they had all rejected me. I realised that I had to be thick-skinned. I got a scholarship which enabled me to continue studying at university in Tokyo. There, I toured magazine editorials, showing my portfolio to hundreds of picture editors. I developed friendships with some of them, which only a knowledge of Japanese could bring, and Vogue offered me a part-time job! It's curious that so many flimsy magazines turned me down but that Vogue took me on.

My university course enriched my photographic work, giving me an insight into Japanese culture – I learnt about woodblock prints and had access to useful materials; I was inspired by theatrical props, sets, kimonos and costumes, which gave me original ideas for shoots. Now that I'm back in London, it's great to have this edge over other photographers. I took a big risk by going into such a competitive field without the usual five-year photography school background, but in fact I benefited from having absorbed a different culture.

My academic and artistic sides complemented each other in other ways. To learn Japanese characters, I included them in paintings. I also hung up huge sheets of paper in my room – my housemates thought I was crazy – and drew all the characters I knew on my walls. Images have such a lasting effect on memory that being constantly surrounded by them served me well in my exams, where I did best in writing and character recognition.

I realised it wouldn't matter how I performed academically, because what was relevant to my photography was that I could speak Japanese – no one would care whether I'd read books about Confucius. However, at a place like Oxford, you keep hearing how difficult it is to get a First, so I made that my goal because I wanted to feel I had no limits. It's true that I had doubts when I saw how capable other students were, and a voice in my head would say, 'They're doing better than you', but there's a Japanese saying which translates as 'positive competition' and I took the view that when you compete with classmates, everybody benefits. So I kept pushing the doubts away.

In fact, without doubts I might have been complacent, whereas the competition pushed me beyond my comfort zones. I had a tutorial partner who wrote essays that blew me away. I was scared by her talent. Actually, 'scared' isn't the right word: I was in awe, and that inspired me to learn from her. I'd think, next tutorial it will be my turn and I want to come up with something that's every bit as good.

I never really had ups and downs – my motivation grew as my Japanese improved. I've always had objectives: at school, to get enough points to get into Oxford, then at Oxford, to learn set characters and finish yearly reading lists. I'd made a commitment to study, a decision that involved making sacrifices since it allowed space only for my closest friends and the most important activities.

I'm proud that I made the most of Oxford. I managed to prove to myself and my family – people I love, that I have a duty to – that I'm able to do something with my life. I thought I'd be worth more if I could achieve intellectually. I'd been given a chance, and I didn't see any point in doing things half-heartedly: I wanted to do my best. I thought I would make myself happy if I got a First.

At the same time, I didn't feel I had anything to lose even if I failed. My main objective being fluency, I took other language exams alongside finals – a language proficiency test and a Japanese speech contest organised by the School of Oriental and African Studies (SOAS). I didn't want first prize, a trip to Japan: I'd already been five times. My sights were set on the second prize, a laptop. I got it and now I use it for all my photography work.

I was never very good at writing essays. English isn't my mother tongue and at the International School I wasn't taught how to write essays the way Oxford expected them. My tutor kept telling me my essays lacked structure and were too muddled. I got a First thanks to my language skills and my factual and cultural knowledge, not my essay skills. In spite of having spent three of my Oxford years practising skeleton essays, I didn't improve hugely. It wasn't a big disappointment because the greater embarrassment would have been not being able to speak Japanese. When you know what you want to do, you can stop what's not important from getting in your way.

Of course, you never know if you're making the right choice, but I decided to throw myself into my career. I'd seen other photographers' work and knew I could do better. So I didn't have any career doubts, though I was scared of the big city and of having to cope without a stable income. My parents – though they believed in me and were happy that I'd found my vocation – were also extremely worried about how I'd manage financially. And who knows, in ten years' time I might want to do something else. All I know is that right now it's the most consuming passion ever.

Although Frederic enjoyed a rather lucky start at a good school, he did not come from a particularly academic background. His account shows the crucial part his attitude played in firing his academic success, and later, his career success. At various points, Frederic met with disappointment, but he had sufficient emotional buoyancy not to respond self-destructively. He couldn't pursue his painting – but rather than give up art altogether, he took up photography instead. He built up his photographic skills by providing services for free. He didn't lose heart despite 50 written rejections – he just concluded, rightly, that he needed to develop a tough attitude given the vagaries of the industry, and tried again in a more direct way.

On the academic side, he had to deal with the considerable problem that his essays were criticised throughout his university career. Given his high standards, he might have taken this as a huge blow and panicked about the consequences. But he used various strategies to cope with his handicap. First, he contextualised: he reminded himself that English was not his first language, and that he hadn't been trained in the British way of writing essays. Second, he tried to improve. Third, he took the sanguine view that the outcome didn't really matter and that he had compensatory skills.

His comment about Confucius is interesting. Even the brightest students need their defences against intellectual challenges. So despite Frederic's proclaimed sense of duty and respect for others, at Oxford he survived with a measured degree of scorn – namely, that he didn't need to master Confucius because he had an alternative career lined up.

A superficial reading of Frederic's testimonial portrays a workaholic obsessed with success: needing to 'do my best', score a First, take additional exams, out-rival fellow students and photographers . . . in short, trying to prove the impossible, that he has 'no limits'. One could worry, particularly having read the first chapter of this book, that someone with such extravagant aims must be setting themselves up for disappointment.

Look more closely and, again, Frederic's account shows a different side. He focused rather more on passion and rather less on the more illusory trappings of success such as grades and money. He rationalised his fears: recall when he corrected the word 'scared' to the more empowering word 'awed'. He liked being top, but he was also pragmatic: second prize could be better. He also decided he could cope even if he failed his degree, a liberating attitude that enabled him to put in the necessary hard graft for a First. And Frederic's enthusiasm drove him to work creatively, to take ownership of his work: he devised some original and extremely effective revision strategies.

Despite occasional failures, Frederic accumulated successful follow-through, gaining confidence. He broke down his large ambitions into manageable and carefully considered goals such as scoring enough points to get into Oxford, picking the most appropriate (rather than the most prestigious) college and mastering Japanese step by step. He felt a duty to his parents, but above all he seems motivated by dignity, as well as by key victories along the way.

Frederic's luck lies mostly in his family background. He refers to his parents as 'really good', 'kind' and 'forward-thinking'. Perhaps there's political correctness in these expressions of gratitude, but it's also clear that Frederic's upbringing gave him strong self-respect, which he extends to others.

Frederic mentioned to me that his father left his mother in his second year at Oxford and that he comforted her by taking beautiful pictures of her. This suggests a relationship between the two of them in which he felt able to exert considerable influence. Frederic is someone who trusts that the world will respond to his actions, and that his efforts will bear fruit.

Maria: too much emotional and academic baggage

Maria qualified as graphic designer in 1996 in Columbia and came to England in 1998. Her testimonial outlines a typical study difficulty, intensified in her case by the pressures of being a mature student.

I was always a very good pupil at school in Columbia. But I was not very happy. My father died suddenly in a car accident when I was a teenager. He used to help me with my school work. He was better educated than my mother. She was quite a tough woman. Life became more difficult because there wasn't very much money after my father died.

Even after my father's death, I continued working hard at school and still got top grades. But now I realise I was taught in quite a mechanical way, learning by heart instead of thinking for myself. At university, most of my work was on computer, with very little work on paper. It didn't matter that I didn't really know how to write essays because we were assessed mainly on our design skills.

It isn't easy to get work in Columbia so I decided to look for work abroad. In 2000 I got full-time work in England. I wanted to consolidate a career in Design and Technology and applied for a Master's degree. It was a three-year course and involved a lot of essay writing in the third year, where I am at now.

My way of working is quite intensive and I noticed that I am much slower than other people with written work. One page of A4 can take me all weekend. When I was in Columbia I had no other time pressures and I could take as long as I needed to study. Now, I have to balance the academic side of my life with my full-time job. So I find it very tiring and stressful not knowing how to study efficiently and it has been a strain in my private life, particularly in my relationship with my partner as we have so little time together – all we have together is evenings and weekends, usually the only time I have to study. I go to bed late and I have to get up early for my day job.

When I am given an essay to write I read as much as I can, which takes a long time, especially when I am tired and find it difficult to take in information. When I come across passages that seem useful to my essay title, I make notes. Usually that means copying out sentences, maybe small paragraphs from books, cutting and pasting passages from online journals into a blank file, or photocopying and highlighting. I often end up with lots and lots of notes – maybe 30 pages. That's the first stage. In the second stage I have to try and organise all these sentences and paragraphs into something that will fit in an essay. It is so difficult knowing where to start that I often feel like tearing all the pages up! I get very angry and tearful. I try numbering or colour-coding paragraphs as a way of grouping together sections that could go next to each other in my essay. But I have so many pieces of paper that I easily get lost in all the detail and very discouraged.

To imagine what the essay will look like as a whole I sometimes cut up my notes into lots of strips and lay them out on my floor. I move the strips around until I think I have a 'best fit', something that flows. I'm not always very confident that I am answering the question enough so I find it hard to prioritise and leave anything out.

The third stage is typing everything into the computer. Usually the essay is much too long, so then there is a fourth stage where I have to cut and rewrite, rewrite, rewrite. Often I am still doing more reading to cover the subject and have more notes to include in the essay. It's very laborious.

For one piece of coursework I had to find an essay title on my own. I had done a lot of reading so I had a lot of notes. But I just couldn't think of the right title for my essay, something that could cover everything I had in my notes. I kept crossing out different versions. After five hours I was crying, 'What's wrong with you, no one else has these problems'. I was panicking about running out of time so I just started writing the essay. Again, I thought nothing I was putting down on paper was up to standard and I just managed a small paragraph when I was supposed to be writing a 3,000-word essay. All that for a whole weekend's work! Now I'm waiting to hear from my tutor to see if she can extend the deadline. But I still have two more essays to write and even less time now than I had before.

I'm not used to getting bad results. I expect really good marks of myself, like the marks I got at school. But I don't know how to do it. My tutors make comments on my work like, 'I'm not sure you've really answered the question', 'You need to draw out the key issues more clearly', 'More analysis and comment needed' or 'This is a really interesting topic and you've clearly undertaken a considerable amount of research but your work is too descriptive and lacks argument'. My methods worked well at school, but now I work twice as hard as other people for half the marks. I don't know what's wrong with me. My GP prescribed anti-depressants and six sessions of cognitive behavioural therapy but I'm not sure if I should go ahead, especially as the pills will take a few months to work, which will be too late to help me with my deadline. I cry a lot and I wonder whether I should give up.

Although the situation sounds desperate, students like Maria don't usually have to give up, with access to the right help. As Maria suspects, pills aren't the answer here since they won't teach her how to write essays. She needs better study skills, and fast, because she is tackling her studies in entirely the wrong way.

School often doesn't prepare children for the challenges they will face at university. Because Maria got excellent marks, she didn't strike her tutors as needing urgent help at university level. But writing at higher levels requires an investigative and independent approach, and some people find that this takes practice.

Because Maria's study problems are typical of many university students' difficulties, I shall detail the approach I took with her to help her complete her overdue coursework essay – the one for which she couldn't find a title.

I worked with Maria for two two-hourly sessions. My first objective was to lower her standards. I asked her just to aim for a pass. She needed enough points to get her MA, nothing more. That took considerable pressure off her, enabling her to get started without feeling compelled to do more reading and research. She also agreed to stop trying to write a comprehensive essay. Tutors and examiners don't expect students to write everything about the subject in a few thousand words: they expect to see a piece of coursework that deals competently with just one small aspect of the course.

It may, at first, feel utterly terrifying, and far too risky to leave out material that could possibly be relevant: the typical trap Maria fell into was to try and make notes on everything, then to cram all her notes into what is actually quite a small word count. Three thousand words seemed like a lot to Maria. But breaking it down, she saw that an introduction and conclusion might use up 250 words each, leaving only 2,500 words for the main part of the essay – space to make about five main points at 500 words each. Five hundred words get eaten up very quickly once you've stated your point and started backing it up, analysing it or commenting on it.

To help Maria develop more trust in her ability, I asked her to tell me what her coursework essay was about. She talked quite spontaneously for ten minutes and realised that she knew enough about the subject to fill her essay without needing her notes. Talking in this way also gave her the overview needed to plan her essay. This formed the basis of a plan, which we restricted to a sheet of A4 (any more and Maria would have been compelled to write something far too detailed, losing sight of the wood for the trees, and ending up with just more notes).

At this point, the essay title started to suggest itself, and we focused on thinking up a specific question that the essay could answer. (Statements tend to be too general to spark a well-argued essay.)

Maria was able to write the essay mostly from memory, in just a few days. Her essay was still too heavy on source material and light on argument and analysis, but she passed and got one step closer to her MA.

Half of our success was due to the fact that Maria was no longer alone in her studies and had me there to help her talk through her essay. I sensed a connection between her tears when trying to study in isolation and her unresolved grief over her father's sudden death. She never had a chance to say goodbye to him. After the shock of his death, Maria was given no time to stop: she continued with school work and exams, under the aegis of a 'tough' mother. Given that her father used to play a very helpful role in her academic work, every time Maria sat at her desk she must have been reminded, consciously or not, of her loss.

Maria was prescribed cognitive behavioural therapy by her doctor. Students who seem depressed are often prescribed this therapy because it's quick (usually requiring only half a dozen sessions) and therefore cheap. The therapy aims to give the client a boost by encouraging positive thinking. In the long term, however, this tends not to help people who have suffered a childhood trauma such as bereavement, abuse or parental divorce, the kinds of issues that need to be talked through and require working through many emotional stages. (Grieving, for instance, is thought to arouse a succession of feelings categorised by psychotherapist Elisabeth Kübler-Ross as denial, anger, bargaining, depression and acceptance.) These people need time and space, and the opportunity to express themselves freely: initially they may feel too upset to get on with their life and their studies. But it is a healthy depression, though it may not seem like it, and leads to recovery. Maria told me that she would get in touch with a bereavement counsellor over the summer.

Andy: exam trauma, career success

Andy, aged 40, is a postgraduate with a 2:2 from Liverpool University and an MSc in Information Technology. To his own astonishment, despite a terror of exams, his relatively modest academic achievements landed him a lucrative and stimulating career managing software development teams for an investment bank.

I suppose I could blame my school a bit for what went wrong. It was a very average comprehensive – OK, quite big, not highly academic, struggling to meet the needs of its pupils. My O-level grades were almost directly proportional to class size – that makes an enormous difference. In all the years I was there the school didn't even have a library! For six months of my A-level preparation, we had no physics teacher. No one taught me study skills and I think it was a bit of surprise how much of a leap A-level was from O-level.

Someone I met later, who'd been to a private school, said his school organised O-levels a year early, so pupils spent three years instead of two preparing A-levels. That format would have suited me better. People develop at different rates. As I got older I got more distracted, spent more time with my friends. I wasn't a particularly mature or prepared 18-year-old. It still embarrasses me to admit it.

Another contributory factor is that although my parents weren't exactly working class, they weren't academic. Also, my mother is Syrian, so when I was young I had less English vocabulary than my classmates. But I was lucky that it was quiet at home, and unlike a lot of people I knew, I had my own room to study in – otherwise I doubt I'd have managed.

I'm quite a nervous person. In an exam, it's borderline whether I can cope. I go to jelly and I'm so nervous that all I can think about is being scared. I can't recall anything. My A-level subjects, Pure Maths, Physics and Economics, involved a lot of problem-solving, which was particularly difficult as I just ended up re-reading the exam questions hundreds of times instead of relaxing and getting into it.

So I got two Ds and an E, not enough to get into university. I wanted to go to Liverpool. It was terrible not getting in. I really worried that I was never going to go anywhere. My parents were really good about it. That was really key. They could have said or done all kinds of hurtful things, like been upset or angry or made me feel I'd disappointed them. They didn't do any of that. Still, it's a major disappointment when you don't succeed at what you want to do, particularly when you compare yourself to your peers. You get it into your head that your age matters when in fact it doesn't – your grades matter when you have conditional offers, but at the time I thought I had to jump this hoop at 16, that hoop at 18 because that's how everyone else did it.

My parents gave me free rein to choose what to do next and I decided to resit my A-levels at a sixth-form college and reapply to Liverpool. In fact my retake year turned out to be really helpful. People change a lot when they go to university, so resitting meant growing apart from my peers, but I made new friends. I could also relax, knowing that I only had to do a little bit better, which made me less nervous in the exams. Liverpool were good: they liked the fact that they were my first choice university and they gave me another chance. I got in on two Cs and a B. My B was in Physics, the subject that mattered least, that I was most relaxed about, because I was dropping it.

I remember my first day at Liverpool like it was yesterday. It seemed unbelievable, like winning the lottery: having failed first time made it so special to be there. I kept giggling with excitement. Overall I had a fantastic time. I got to live the fun life of a student, away from home, mixing with like-minded people and people from very mixed backgrounds. There were mature students, or people who'd never got A-levels but whose studies were being sponsored by their company. One of them worked for a power supplier, and he just had a City & Guilds qualification. Then at the other end of my corridor there was another guy who was a top student reading medicine. Some people sneered at my academic record but the majority didn't care – theirs wasn't any better. So what I'd imagined was really important in life, the expectations I had about how things should be, turned out to be totally wrong. That gave me confidence.

Academically, I struggled at times. I regard myself as being terrible in exam situations, and there were some desperately worrying moments . . . in pretty much all my exams, in fact. And it's daunting and frustrating when other people put in less effort and go further than you. For instance, some people I met at Liverpool had an astounding standard of English, and although I did improve my written English, I've only become confident with it since leaving university. And the medicine guy, for instance, didn't do more work than me yet, unlike me, seemed to remember everything he learnt. But what carried me was that I found the work interesting. When you really like a subject, it makes such a difference. Some people might think it a good idea to pick subjects just for their status value, but doing something you enjoy might make all the difference between a pass and a fail. I was really interested in my dissertation topic, and because that was a large part of my degree, it got me through.

Also, I got support from university that I never got from my school. It makes a big difference when people have time and inclination to help you out, and Liverpool made a real effort that way. It's a university that prides itself on taking in people from all walks of life and local people especially. Once you're in, it doesn't matter who you are or what you're doing, they'll do what they can for you. The lecturers were always willing to offer information if I asked them after lectures, and there was one-to-one help available from my personal tutor.

I hoped for a 2:1 because it feels like that's the dividing line between success and failure. I got a 2:2, which is pretty much what I'd scored all the way through my time at university. I was worried because I knew my degree would relate to my job prospects – and after graduating I was unemployed for a year.

Then I was fortunate to get onto an MSc course in Information Technology. At the time there was a big push on IT, which provided lots of opportunities. That changed everything: suddenly I was hot stuff. I've been very lucky – I just needed a couple of breaks, which were getting into Liverpool, doing the MSc, and then eventually getting a job in an investment bank.

Different careers have different expectations of your academic performance. In my experience, the hard bit is getting a foot in the door, and also when you change jobs your grades matter a bit, but after that, what counts is how you do the job.

As if to prove that, my bank gives staff private access to a digitised copy of their CV on computer and when I looked up mine, I noticed that all that they took account of was my subjects, not my grades: 'degree – yes; further degree – yes'. They use a formula to work out your market value and your pay packet, according to your age and experience. I had it in my head that I'd get paid less because I'd only got a 2:2. I was wrong.

I'm in constant competition with colleagues who have very strong academic backgrounds. Generally I'm fine, but there are moments when it can be difficult. I don't reveal my own background. I wouldn't give people the opportunity to embarrass me or put me down. A small part of me sometimes thinks I don't deserve . . . but academic record isn't always a good indicator of ability. And experience has taught me that if you really want to do something and you suffer major setbacks it doesn't necessarily mean you can't do it. I've hired people from all backgrounds, many of whom have praised me for what they assume to be my academic achievements. I let them carry on believing it.

I realise now that my working life is cyclical, with ups and downs. You can ride a wave of success – it's self-fuelling, and then you just keep getting better; whereas if you stumble and stall it can be hard to recover and stop that backward trend. I've experienced both first-hand.

Yet often if I put myself forward for something that feels out of my depth, then bizarrely, something comes from it. For instance, when I applied for my current job through an agency, I didn't realise till after I'd applied that it was a team-leading position: amazingly, I got the job. The interview was nerve-racking but I probably came across as being relaxed, because I wasn't expecting to be selected, and I told myself it didn't matter.

I've learnt another thing: work offers further opportunities to learn more, beyond your degree. When you get your finals result you think, that's it, that's my badge, but you can progress beyond that and acquire specialist skills that increase your professional standing. It takes the pressure off your degree, but I didn't realise that at the time.

Andy's account hardly needs much comment, other than that it sums up many major themes laid out in this book.

He suffered from typical stresses that many students will relate to: unfavourable comparisons with peers, a constant sense of failure, a terror of not jumping through hoops and of falling by the wayside.

Fortunately, he had just enough tenacity to hang on and keep trying. He saw the good in what other people might consider to be bad: partly by making new friends, he turned his retake year into a positive experience despite the stigma of having failed. He also recognised that it was doing him good to have an extra year in which to prepare his A-levels. At university, he used all the help available to him to improve his work. His account illustrates the point that I make in Chapter 1, that although in the short term exam results may make a difference, in the long run it is attitude that matters more.

However worrying it may be to underperform as a student, the qualities required to do well in exams and those required do well in a career bear little relation to each other. Although throughout his student days, Andy was inhibited by his fear of exams, this has not affected his working performance, despite the fact that he works in a competitive and stressful environment.

It's not because Andy has changed and can cope better with being tested. He still gets nervous in certain situations. For instance, he found it so nerve-racking being best man at his brother's wedding that he nearly blacked out when he had to deliver his speech. No one noticed. There are many people like Andy around, who die a thousand deaths in secret but appear to be coping perfectly well to others around them. Andy is one of those people who give others the impression that he doesn't have any problems.

I asked Andy what stopped him from falling apart entirely in exams. His response was that it was a close thing. At school, he had known a boy who did brilliantly in his O-levels, and then suffered a breakdown prior to taking his A-levels. Andy didn't think it would have taken much for him to suffer the same fate.

What Andy had, though, was the staunch support of his parents. His failure revealed that their loyalty to him was not performance related, and that their love therefore ran deeper than he might otherwise have imagined. The fact that Andy refers to this as 'key' suggests that he felt it was his parents' solidarity that most helped him unlock his potential.

Emily: apathy and disorganisation

Emily graduated from Cambridge University with a 2:1 in English. Now, 20 years later, she works as a part-time copy editor and free-lance journalist and is married with two children under 5. Here she reflects on the reasons behind her lack of motivation as a student, the stress that she underwent in making the grade, and questions the value of an educational path ill-fitted to her needs.

I went to a large boarding school with academically high standards. It was the kind of place where they display league tables of high achievers and low achievers and frogmarch you through the exam system. Teachers had financial incentives to get good grades out of their pupils. For a couple of terms we had weekly study skills lessons in which we did practice essay plans on general topics, just to get the hang of organising our thoughts on paper. From dawn to dusk, we were completely regulated by the school timetable: mealtimes, lesson times, homework times, and bed-times were set in stone. Nothing was left to chance.

Like most people, I was pretty scared of exams but I was trained to do well in them. I got high grades, mostly As. But I didn't enjoy school – not at all. There was a bad atmosphere in my boarding house, quite a lot of bullying, and no moral support from the adults who were supposed to be acting *in loco parentis*. We were there to work and score. I started out very eager about the school (I had first visited it as a 10-year-old with my parents on a lovely sunny day, and the buildings looked beautiful). You could be forgiven for thinking that the system had been designed to strip all enthusiasm for learning out of its pupils. Within months we had all become bored with the work routine and the constant pressure of having to achieve. There was nothing pedagogical about the way the school was run. If you did well, you got prizes; if you did badly, you got publicly humiliated.

After my A-levels I went straight to Cambridge University to read English. It felt pretty much like boarding school all over again, except that now I was suddenly expected to be self-motivated and devoted to my subject. I wasn't. I was bored and frustrated by much of the syllabus. I would have liked to study a few contemporary authors, but the course started with Old English and involved an enormous amount of dull translation work in the first year. I can't say I cared much about Old English poetry. I was tired of working.

I kept hearing this rumour that it's almost impossible to fail your first year exams. So I didn't see any reason to organise myself, create revision schedules, read books or even go to lectures. Lectures, all voluntary, were far too specialised anyway: they fitted the very narrow field of research conducted by the lecturer, not the more general requirements of my syllabus. As for my tutors, most of them really didn't seem to give a stuff about teaching undergraduates. For them, the point of being at Cambridge was to do research. Teaching was just an occupational hazard that went with the job.

I procrastinated and watched a lot of television in my bedroom. I also got involved in producing and directing student drama productions. I'd always been interested in drama: at Cambridge there was lots going on. I started to feel like I was on a drama course with a bit of English on the side.

My revision consisted of reading basic A-level guides to my set texts.

I sat the exams completely unprepared . . . and failed.

I can't describe the shock of failing. I'd never failed an exam in my life. I'd always been a straight-A student. Suddenly, my Cambridge career was hanging on a knife-edge. If I failed resits, that was it: I would get kicked out. I didn't think there would be any future for me if that happened.

That summer, I stayed in Portugal with my family. They went to the beach: I worked indoors.

In September I resat, and passed. Just. But the experience of having failed my first year exams haunted me for the rest of my two years at university. I became extremely anxious about assessments. The joy I could have had, particularly in my last year, was overshadowed by the thought of having to sit finals. To make matters worse, my college room overlooked the Examinations Hall so my last few months were spent staring in horror at other students going through the ordeal. I took caffeine pills, smoked like crazy and developed huge bags under my eyes. My boyfriend – now my husband – urged me to take more time off, but I only felt reassured about my prospects when I was working. Once I fell asleep in the library and realised when I woke half an hour later that I'd drooled all over a reference book. Then I looked about me and saw that everyone else in the library was also asleep. Probably also drooling.

My problem wasn't with exam technique. I was good at that. What I didn't have, which is where I think I'm fairly typical of many students, was enough knowledge of the subject. I just wasn't interested enough. I look at my children and how much they love learning. For them, it's exciting and fun. It's heartbreaking to think that I must have started that way too. But from age 11 to 21, I was put through every kind of exam: eleven O-levels, two S-levels, three A-levels, then my first year exams, resits, then finals. That's upwards of 19 major exams in just five years. At the end of it, I was getting constant finals nightmares, about sitting exams and having absolutely no preparation. I was also insomniac. I came out of university vowing that I would never, ever sit another exam in my life.

I honestly don't think Cambridge was much use for me. Of course, I'm glad I met my husband there. On a general note, university taught me a rigorous way of thinking, writing and researching, so I'm glad of that despite the fact you'll never catch me reading a classic again. Cambridge also got me seriously involved in drama, something that I carried on doing after I left. I directed a few professional productions in my mid to late twenties. Then I started to burn out from that and took up copy-editing – dull, but regular paid work. Now, I'm over 40 and just scraping my way into journalism. The problem I've always suffered is not being trained in anything. Following university, I couldn't bear the prospect of doing one more day's studying. Everything I've done I've had to learn on the job, and I've constantly felt like an impostor. Because I'm good at what I do, and I can think on my feet, no one has yet found me out. But all in all, I don't think I benefited from all that academic stress.

I wasn't a rebellious teenager. I didn't see any reason to turn against a system that was rewarding me, where I was being patted on the head and told that I was doing well. The prospect of having all that stripped away was quite frightening. My application to Cambridge consisted of flicking through the handbook wondering what course to choose, until a teacher suggested English. I was just following the path I'd been led down, oblivious to the fact I could do something else. So I did what I was told, worked hard and then couldn't really cope with the consequences.

You should really only go to a place like Cambridge if you want to do one of their courses, because going to a top university is no panacea. It's a lot of heartache and hard work. Yes, it looks good on your CV but what use is that if by the time you've graduated you're too exhausted and run down to do anything useful? There were lots of people like me who just ended up drifting after their degree. I'd have done better to opt for a vocational course, perhaps in journalism, or to try and get into drama or film school. Or I should have got a job and gone to university later, when I was more mature. No one told me that at the time. All the educational establishments I went through encouraged students to think that the best thing anyone could do in life was to head for the top of the academic league table, and fast. I don't think that kind of education had much to do with real life.

I had a conversation with a Cambridge don in which I told him how much I envied him. Surely he was teaching some of the most motivated students in the country, maybe even in the world. And surely that must be just wonderful. To my surprise, he looked extremely downcast. His response was that his students were mostly uninterested in academia. Yes, they had been desperate to get the best grades at A-level, in order to get into Cambridge. But once they were in, the last thing these A-grade students wanted to do was more work.

Emily's account bears this out, and explains some of the reasons behind this sad phenomenon. But I don't think that the academic burn-out she describes is particular only to high achievers. It seems to me that years of studying and being tested can wear down pupils and students at every level. In our increasingly league-table-driven educational climate, state schools are also beginning to turn the screw on their pupils who now sit tests from the tender age of seven. At least Emily got a privileged education, good grades and was branded a success, which must surely have been a less stressful experience than that of pupils who are tested just as much but branded failures.

It is a well-known cause for concern that many university lecturers forget students to concentrate on research (partly because they compete with each other to receive funding for their projects) – a phenomenon publicly deplored by one academic, Lord May, who in a 2003 address to the Royal Society, commented that it was becoming almost a mark of status in some places to have a minimum engagement with undergraduates. Ironically, this tends to happen most in high-ranking universities such as Oxford and Cambridge where the famous one-on-one tutorial tradition ought to foster greater rather than lesser understanding between staff and students.

Even more ironically, the most privileged students who attend these high-ranking universities are more likely to need study support than students with similar A-level grades but who have more mainstream educational backgrounds. A study of almost 50,000 students conducted in 2005 by academics at Warwick University found that boys, in particular, who attend the most expensive public schools, are the most likely to underperform at university – with a direct link between higher fee levels and lower finals results (every £2,000 increase in school fees was found to correlate with one percentage point less in higher education achievement compared with other undergraduates attaining the same A-level grades).

Emily fits well into this pattern, in that she had always got excellent grades, largely because her school drilled her, and so never thought of herself as a possible candidate for failure. She went from a school where she was organised to the tiniest detail, and made to do her homework every night under supervised conditions, to a university where she was (more or less) free to do exactly what she liked. Quite typically, she turned her back on academia and immersed herself in extracurricular activities at the expense of her studies, unaware of the impact this would have on her academic career. Rather like a caged animal suddenly set loose and having no idea how to survive in the wild, the consequence was a dangerous one and, despite her intelligence and her academic prowess, she nearly ruined her higher education.

Emily makes an important comment about the value of teenage rebellion. Perhaps she would have done better to question the system a little more, and take some risks. The rewards of academic success were an enticement away from her own path, which explains why sometimes rebels and drop-outs do better in the long run. One striking example of this paradox is TV newsreader Jon Snow. Like Emily, he was privately educated at boarding school. He initially failed one A-level out of two, then only got D and E in a second attempt at A-levels, at a technical college. Sick of studying, he left England for the first time in his life, to spend a year in Uganda teaching English, a life-changing experience: 'I was a sort of compressed unimaginative Tory when I went out there and I came back a rebel.' This new streak got him into trouble when he returned to his studies: during his second year at Liverpool, studying Law – a place he obtained by the skin of his teeth, after visiting the university admissions service in person – he became involved in an anti-apartheid protest about the university's investment in South Africa, which got him kicked out. But in doing so, he did persuade the then university chancellor, Lord Salisbury, to resign. From there, he went to London and became the director of New Horizon Youth Centre, a charity for homeless children, run by Lord Longford. Three years and still no degree later, he got a job on LBC radio as a talk-show host, a career move that eventually led to the position he holds now at Channel Four. 'Toil in hope and you will get there,' he says.

The challenge for students like Emily, whose capacity for toil has long died away, is to regain their motivation. Certainly, going straight from her regimented school to university, Emily would have fared better in an establishment that offered her some closer supervision. The more contemporary courses offered by less prestigious universities might have suited her better too. Students need to be on a course they find as stimulating and interesting as possible, but sometimes even that's not enough, if the student is very burnt out. It's often overlooked how exhausted young people can be by decades of schooling. Sometimes a gap year is the answer, just to provide breathing space, but as Emily points out, it may be better in some cases to take a longer break and consider university at a later stage in life.

The conclusion I draw is a very simple one. There is no set way to be successful in your work. It helps to have motivation and study skills. But studying is so complex, and involves so many factors to do with attitudes and emotions, that you can be a straight-A student at school, yet be challenged at university in ways you never expected. Or you can struggle to find your feet all the way through your academic life and still get a terrific job at the end of it. People shouldn't feel under too much pressure to follow a preordained path, churn out top grades and jump through academic hoops at particular times in their life. Knowing this, the majority of students would panic less, find work less stressful, enjoy their subjects more and – paradoxically – perform better.

Appendix 1: Coursework and exam checklist

★ ## As early as possible

Organise special exam provisions, if applicable ☐

Check you have an up-to-date syllabus ☐

Get other useful documentation which is not available without asking (examiners' reports, mark schemes, past papers, past coursework, model answers) ☐

Put coursework deadlines into a calendar or planner ☐

Put exam dates into a calendar or planner ☐

Order equipment for oncoming practicals or presentations, if applicable ☐

★ ## About two months before your exams

Timetable exam revision ☐

Organise time off work, if applicable ☐

Organise childcare, if applicable ☐

★ ## About a fortnight before your exams

Timetable past paper practice ☐

★ The day before

Check exam venue ☐

Prepare exam clothes (or sub fusc if required – for example if you are an Oxford or Cambridge University student) ☐

Prepare food (breakfast and exam snacks/drinks) ☐

Check equipment and batteries, if applicable ☐

★ Other

Book a holiday, perhaps? ☐

☐

☐

☐

Appendix 2: Save time at your computer

It's thought that 80 per cent of computer users understand only 20 per cent of their software capability. In some cases this may well be a blessing – messing about with finer features can waste a lot of time. (The temptation is to spend ages fiddling with coursework presentation even though this is rarely worth very many marks.)

However, it's worth knowing about features that really do ease your workload. Assuming that you are among the majority who use Microsoft Word as a word-processing package and Windows as an operating system, here are some basic functions you might want to get acquainted with if you're not using them already. Most of these are on your toolbar; for more information on these or other time-saving functions, press F1 to get the 'Help' menu and type in your search.

Whatever system you use, look for the equivalent of the features listed below.

- Spellcheck
- Word count
- Cut and paste
- Draft printing
- Mouse features (e.g. triple-click to select a paragraph; right-click for dropdown options; select and drag to cut and paste)
- Keyboard functions ('Home'; 'End'; F7 = spell check)
- Word keyboard shortcuts (Ctrl + S = save a document; Ctrl + N = create a new document; Ctrl + C/X/V = Copy/Cut/Paste)
- Windows keyboard shortcut (Alt + F4 = close program; Microsoft Key + D = minimise all windows)
- Pagination
- Tables
- Fields (formulae by which your computer makes calculations with figures you enter in a table)
- Styles (e.g. change all heading styles in one go)
- Document map (lists a menu of your headings as you work – useful for long pieces of work)
- Headers and footers; making footnotes

- Page view (useful before printing) and cancel printing
- Switch off automatic spelling and grammar
- tOGGLE cASE and other case changes
- Undo or repeat typing (reverses changes you just made)
- Margins
- Find and replace
- Cross-referencing
- Flag words (e.g. for index or bibliography)
- Macros (mini-programs that instantly carry out repetitive tasks – these are preset, e.g. 'remove all document frames'; or you can create your own)
- Autotext (programs that recognise your abbreviations, e.g. you write 'photosy', your computer writes 'photosynthesis')
- Automatic Index and Contents functions

Three golden rules

Aside from that, there are three golden rules when using computers for coursework:

> 1 Save as you write.
>
> 2 Back everything up (use a Zip drive or CD writer to store large amounts of data).
>
> 3 Always use the spellcheck and make this the last thing you do before you print.

Finally, a word about spellchecks. They are a useful tool but do have a weakness: they don't find wrong words that are spelt correctly. Therefore, before doing a spellcheck, proofread your work. To do this successfully, you're best off printing a rough copy, as errors on paper tend to be easier to spot than on the screen.

Appendix 3: Second chances

I include this section not because I think anything will go wrong – on the contrary, if you use the ideas in this book, your exams are likely to go smoothly – but because it's often useful to know that if the worst came to the worst and you did fail in some way, you could still have a second chance.

 ## Appeals

Finals papers are usually marked by two examiners. In cases where there is a discrepancy between results, a third marker will normally be called upon to adjudicate. Therefore, it's extremely unlikely that your exam result will not reflect your performance. If, however, you do have reason to doubt the fairness of the marking, your first port of call is your senior tutor, who may make an official complaint to the exam board.

 ## Resits

You would normally resit automatically if you failed your first year modular or preliminary papers. At finals level, you can't resit a First, Second or Third class honours degree. However, if you receive an unclassified degree, an aegrotat (see Appendix 5) or a fail, you should, in principle, be eligible to repeat the year.

Among the student population who sat finals at Oxford University in 1999, only 0.4 per cent failed to get an honours degree – I hope this puts exam failure into perspective. In the extremely unlikely event that this happened to you, you could still resit if you wished, and, technically, complete your studies with a First. (Check with your college.)

Cheering news.

Appendix 4: Learning difficulties

The greatest problem that comes with a learning difficulty is low academic self-esteem. You may have found it hard to engage with your work, particularly if, as is often the case, you didn't receive adequate backup in your schooling to overcome your difficulty. Your commitment and organisation may be hampered by worries about being different. In this case, consider the following points:

- Everyone is unique. Therefore you are not framed by your diagnosis.
- The boundaries between what are classified as normal and specific learning difficulties can be hazy. Terms like dyslexia or dyspraxia can give the false impression that people can be fitted into neat categories.
- These problems are not always permanent. I see in my work a startling number of cases of children diagnosed once with dyslexia or dyspraxia, whose subsequent tests show no learning difficulty.

A diagnosis has its uses if it enables you to progress in some way. Overcome your problem by stimulating all your senses – use mnemonics, colours and sketches in your revision, and revise frequently, as explained in Chapter 4. Mindmaps can help you revise and plan your coursework. Discussions with friends may also be useful – talking your ideas through may help you formulate your plans.

You can obtain further information and learning support from the Successful Learning centre listed at the end of this book. Your tutor or your student support centre may also offer valuable help. Don't be afraid to seek it.

Appendix 5: Special exam provisions

The first rule is that you shouldn't expect anything to be organised for you. There's no automatic routine, as each university has its own disability statement. Arrangements therefore vary from institution to institution. Your senior tutor can advise you on the normal procedure. You will certainly need to substantiate your claim with a medical certificate (in the case of illness) or an up-to-date educational psychologist's assessment (in the case of a learning difficulty). Do so *as early as possible in the academic year*, so that the exam board has time to make arrangements for you. (I recommend that you keep a photocopy of the certificate you send in case it gets lost in transit.)

Below are some typical situations for which special arrangements are normally made. To find out more about allowances that can be made for a range of conditions from dyslexia to blindness, contact Skill, the national bureau for students with disabilities, listed at the end of this book.

 ## Learning difficulties

A certificate for a learning difficulty such as dyslexia will normally allow you between 10 and 15 minutes' extra time in the hour – in other words, you can expect an extra 45 minutes in a three-hour paper. If your difficulty is severe you may be given more; you may also be given coloured exam paper and allowed to use a computer with a spellcheck.

Examiners will be advised to make suitable allowances. For dyslexia-style conditions, this would normally mean disregarding spelling irregularities.

 ## Illness or disability

The type of arrangement made for illness or disability varies according to the nature of your condition. For instance, you should be able to sit the exam at your college if the journey to the exam room is too difficult for you, or you may obtain permission to take food into the exam.

If you have a condition such as ME your invigilator will almost certainly be instructed to allow you rest periods during your exam – usually, you might expect a 10 or 15 minute break on the hour as extra time. You might also expect a restriction of the number of exams you sit in any one week.

A tiny minority of students fall seriously ill during their exam period. If anything like appendicitis or severe flu prevents you from completing all your finals papers, you will most likely be eligible for an aegrotat degree, which is an unclassified honours degree. This is awarded to students who have done enough work to qualify for an honours degree but not enough to show which class they fall into – first, second or third. It also comes with the option to resit.

Help with English

If English isn't your mother tongue, you may be given permission to take a bilingual dictionary into your exam (though you will not usually be allowed extra time). You may also be able to receive additional English tuition – check with your student support centre.

Useful addresses

Nutritional advice

British Nutrition Foundation
52–54 High Holborn
London
WC1V 6RQ
Tel: 020 7404 6504
Email: postbox@nutrition.org.uk
www.nutrition.org.uk

Helping with prescription drugs

Counsel for Involuntary Tranquilliser Addiction (CITA)
Helpline: 0151 949 0102
Offers information and counselling for family and friends as well as sufferers.

Help with recreational drugs

National Drugs Helpline: 0800 776600
Release Helpline: 020 7729 9904
www.release.org.uk

Help with alcohol

Drinkline: 0800 917 8282
www.recovery.org.uk
www.wrecked.co.uk

Help with smoking

NHS Smoking Helpline: 0800 1690169
www.givingupsmoking.co.uk

Counselling

The Samaritans: 08457 909090
Email: jo@samaritans.org
www.samaritans.org

British Association for Counselling and Psychotherapy
35–37 Albert Street
Rugby CV21 2SG
Office: 01788 550 899
Email: bacp@bacp.co.uk
www.bacp.co.uk
Offers information on finding a qualified counsellor.

Help with learning difficulties

Successful Learning
36 Caldy Road
West Kirby
Merseyside
CH48 2HQ
Tel: 0151 625 2619

Help with special exam provisions

Skill: National Bureau for Students with Disabilities
Chapter House
18–20 Crucifix Lane
London SE1 3JW
Information Service voice: 0800 328 5050 (freephone)
Voice: 020 7657 2337
Text: 0800 068 2422 (freetext)
Email: Info@skill.org.uk
www.skill.org.uk

Bibliography

In case you wish to follow them up, the publications I refer to in this book are as follows:

DeGrandpre, R. (1999) *Ritalin Nation: Rapid-Fire Culture and the Transformation of Human Consciousness.* New York: Norton.

James, O. (1998) *Britain on the Couch: Why We're Unhappier Than We Were in the 1950s – Despite Being Richer.* London: Random House.

Jeffers, S. (1987) *Feel the Fear and Do It Anyway: Dynamic Techniques for Turning Fear, Indecision and Anger into Power, Action and Love.* London: Arrow Books.

Jones, H. (1997) *Sensual Drugs.* Berkeley, CA: Cambridge University Press.

Layard, R. (2005) *Happiness: Lessons from a New Science.* London: Penguin.

Pam, A. (1990) A critique of the scientific status of biological psychiatry, *Acta Psychiatrica Scandinavica, Supplemental,* 362: 1–35.

Pitchford, P. (1993) *Healing with Whole Foods: Oriental Traditions and Modern Nutrition.* Berkeley, CA: North Atlantic Books.

Here are five other books which you may find interesting or useful:

Buzan, T. (1974) *Use Your Head.* London: BBC Publications.

Fisher Cassie, W. and Constantine, T. (1977) *Students' Guide to Success.* London: Macmillan. Particularly useful for students taking exams in science and engineering.

Pitter, K., Callahan, J., Minato, R., Amato, S. and Pitter, G. (1998) *Every Student's Guide to Life on the Net.* Maidenhead: McGraw-Hill.

Salzberger-Wittenberg, I., Henry, G. and Osborne, E. (1983) *The Emotional Experience of Learning and Teaching.* London: Routledge and Kegan Paul. Explains the unconscious psychological issues that inevitably arise between teacher and learner, helping or hindering the educational process.

Wheeler, M. (1983) *Counselling in Study Methods.* Exeter: University of Exeter Teaching Services. Promoted as a tutors' manual, this book is in my view equally useful for students, as it describes study methods from a counselling perspective, taking into account the emotional aspects of learning at university.

Index

Locators shown in *italics* refer to tables and illustrations.